Written in the Stars

Understanding Astrology and How Your Star Sign Influences Your Life

Kevin Jobson

or indirect, that are incurred as a result of the use of the information contained within this document, including, but not limited to, errors, omissions, or inaccuracies.

Table of Contents

Introduction

Throughout the ages, people have used astrology and star signs to assist them in decisions about their life. Of course, there is no scientific evidence that astrology works or that it has ever worked. But, something that has been around this long and continues to have resonance with people must have something in it, right? Right. After the search for understanding of the stars, is the human race trying to reach some understanding for themselves? Although reading your star sign in the paper is unlikely to be the key to changing your life, sometimes reading your daily astrological advice can suggest things that you had not considered, and so can prove useful in that sense. It must always be read with not just a pinch of salt, but two handfuls at the very least! That doesn't mean that star signs and astrology are bunkum; something that has been around this long has some truth in it. By understanding our star signs and the skies above us, we can begin to understand how we can improve our lives in so many areas.

Ever wondered why you just can't find that right man or woman for you and you keep ending up with the same types that break your heart? Maybe it's because you keep getting together with the wrong star signs, the ones that have the attributes that rub you the wrong way or don't really lend well to fidelity and faithfulness. Or maybe you are in a relationship and you just can't work out why your partner does this one annoying thing, or why they behave and react a certain way to things you do. Understanding your own star sign and the star sign of your partner may help you realize why you are both behaving the way you do and what you can do about it to ensure harmony in the relationship.

Ever wondered why the job you are in just isn't motivating you to do your best? You feel this is not what you were born to do, but equally, you're not really sure what it is you were born to do. Looking at astrology can help you understand what it is you were born to do and help you choose the career that you will find fulfilling and enjoyable. Also, you may be procrastinating about making a move from one company to another, or looking for a promotion, or thinking about asking for a pay rise. Understanding astrology will help you understand exactly when to make the right move at the right time.

It's not just your work where understanding your star sign can help you; it can even help you when choosing your hobbies. Tried to learn to play the piano and found you were just not getting anywhere? You fancy yourself as an artist, but those drawings of stick men really aren't cutting it? Maybe it's because the hobbies you are looking at just aren't suited to the kind of characteristics your star sign has. Understand your star sign, and you can understand exactly what the hobbies are that you should be pursuing. That way, you stand much more chance of being a success at it.

Though nothing beats visiting your doctor or a hospital and by no means should you use your star sign for medical advice, astrology can help you ward off the kind of health complaints your star sign may make you prone to. Having some of the characteristics and attributes associated with your star sign could lead to mental health difficulties or physical difficulties, and better to think them through now and be aware of possible difficulties now than when it is too late. Always work in consultation with your doctor, though, if it leads you to thinking you may want to take any supplements or medication or anything like that as a result. This book will not be providing medical advice, just acting as a guide to what you may be more susceptible to and how to try to counteract those types of things through behaviors and warning signs. It will not offer suggestions of medicines or supplements that you should be taking. You should only consult with your doctor and other medical professionals for medical advice.

You may be thinking, "Well, concentrating on dating and work and hobbies are all very well, but at the moment, I'm living in a town or a city that is still under strict lockdown. I'm really not allowed to move around much at the moment, I can't see my friends other than in a virtual capacity, and I'm not coping at all well with the situation." If that is the case, this last chapter in this book also addresses why that may be. As with the other topics in this book, understanding astrology and your star sign will help you understand why you may not be as well accustomed to coping with the lockdown as other people you know, and may assist with providing suggestions about what you need to do to better cope with the lockdown and the kind of ideas and activities your brain needs to concentrate on to get through these troublesome times with more ease than is currently the case. If you are coping well with the lockdown and the many restrictions that exist around the world because of the pandemic, but you are not really sure why you are coping so well, perhaps studying your star sign can help you appreciate why you are finding it easier than most. This may help you not take that ease for granted and guard against a time when you may not be able to cope so well.

When things stick around for millennia, it is usually with good reason. Even if astrology may not carry the scientific certainty that the human race once believed it did, the lessons and truths that can be found in astrology will always prove useful to people. Sometimes you just need to know when and where to look within astrology to find the advice that can be useful to you. It is almost like looking at an ancient language that you have no knowledge of. If you have a person that can translate it for you, suddenly it comes alive. You can begin to understand it and it makes sense to you, and you can relate it to your own life.

This book acts as your translator to unlock the secrets of the language of astrology and help you understand star signs so that you may use this knowledge to help improve in your life. Don't worry, it is not so difficult to understand that you will feel bemused or bewildered when reading this book. Astrology can be understood without needing to be an astronomer who can spot which stars are which and know the constellations like the back of their hand, or be Nostradamus and be able to predict things in a vague yet detailed way.

This book picks five main areas where you can apply this knowledge to help improve your life, as they are the mainstays of our life and the things we consider the most important. Once you start to study astrology and the star signs, you will get a feel for what your purpose in life is and what behaviors you need to address or lay off of. With that kind of knowledge, you can improve on any area of your life, not just the ones addressed in this book. I would say that it is best not to let astrology rule your life. Personally, and it is just a personal opinion, I think if you get into the realms of postponing your wedding because the moon isn't in the right place on the day you booked, then you start getting into dangerous territory where you can become fearful of life rather than enjoying it.

This book is to help you improve your life, not to make you fearful of it. Astrology is not an exact science; it is not a science at all. So, be wary of those who start saying to you they can predict your future and that you shouldn't eat a cheese sandwich on a Tuesday because it may cause bad karma in your life. That is not a road you want to go down. Enjoy this book, learn from this book, and let it assist you with learning the language of astrology and star signs. Start to take those necessary steps towards improving your life in the areas you want to, and start to become the person you always wanted to be and, more importantly, the person you were always meant to be.

Chapter 1:

What Is Astrology?

Astrology is the analysis of the position in the sky, and the movements within the sky, of the stars, moons and suns, with the belief that such movement and positioning affects the lives of human beings (Astrology, n.d.). The word itself has not deviated too much from its origins of the Greek word for star 'astron,' the Latin word 'astrologia,' and the old French 'astrologie' (Astrology, n.d.) It is not to be confused with astronomy, which is a science that looks at the universe and the objects within it such as stars, but does not believe those objects have a direct impact in daily human lives—unless an asteroid is going to hit our planet, or the moon moves way off course, which would impact the movement of the waves here and could cause tsunamis and the like.

Although it is not a science, the purpose of astrology is still one that holds dear to human life today. That purpose is to understand yourself, accept yourself for who you are, and become the very best you that you can possibly be (Taylor, 2014). What's not to love about that purpose? Every one of us can relate to that; most of us find that is the struggle of our lives. So, you may not become the very best you by reading the daily horoscope in the newspaper where "Mystic Malcolm" advises you not to drink tea on Tuesday, because if you do, none of your friends are going to speak to you for the rest of the month. But, digging into the origins of astrology and star signs and beginning to understand how it all relates to you can really help with thinking about that purpose and using it as a guide to achieving that purpose, and your purpose in life.

The basics of Western astrology, as we know it today, are the 12 star signs of the zodiac we all know and love. There have been controversies that there should be 13. But the truth probably is that it was always known there was a 13th; it just suited us better with our 12 months of the year to stick to 12. We will detail these more in chapter 2 and explain them, but they are also broken down into the four elements: fire, water, air and earth, with three of the signs in each element. Then you also need to be aware of the Sun, the Moon, and all the planets (again, there can be controversies as some astrologers use planets that others don't). Once you know all of this, it is a case of knowing what the person's characteristics are likely to be based on their star sign, and what is happening up in the skies at the moment or in the future, or where everything was at the time the person was born, to be able to suggest the best thing to do in any given situation and what the best way forward might be.

The History of Astrology

Astrology is nearly as old as human civilization itself. The Western version with its star signs can be traced back to the Babylonians in one of the earliest human civilizations, Mesopotamia. They had already been keen astronomers, noticing the sun, moon, planets and stars, who first designed the concept of the zodiac. The zodiac is the order in which the constellations move through the skies, and the Babylonians devised the system which they considered measured celestial time, by dividing that time up into 12 constellations and providing some of the constellations with names of animals. The constellations measure out the time of the year and are related to various gods, which is where it starts to have associations with divine influence, which is the side of astrology we don't want to concentrate on. But, the original concept of the zodiac without the divine aspect is of great interest to us. In fact, it has even proved useful to astronomers. The word zodiac actually comes to us from the Greeks, though. In Greek, it roughly translates as "animal circles" ("History of Astrology," 2020).

This brings us nicely onto the Greeks and Greek speakers as they pick up the divine aspect baton of astrology and run with it following the invasion of Babylon by Alexander the Great, which brings them awareness of the Babylonian astrology, Using their Greek gods makes astrology all the more interesting to the ordinary person on the street, and they also begin to use astrology to suggest it can have an impact on the individual. Previously, the Babylonians had only really been using astrology to suggest how it can best help the whole civilization, not necessarily believing it can have any influence on a specific person. Ptolemy's work *Tetrabiblos* from 140 A.D. is considered one of the most important works on astrology, containing many of the same principles and identifications that are used in astrology today. From Greece, astrology spread out into the Arab world. Baghdad is said to have been built according to the best astrological advice of the day—at the moment that Jupiter, considered the planet of dynasties, was rising in the east and Mars, the planet of war, was setting in the west. Interesting stuff, really. Baghdad is still standing all these years later, just about, so maybe they got it right—although with everything that has happened in its history, maybe not. Maybe they needed to wait for Mars to not only set but run off somewhere else by quite a considerable time!

After the Arab world, astrology got translated back into Latin and proceeded to take over the rest of the Western world, where it is still going strongly, depending on how you look upon it, today. Many leaders throughout the ages are said to have consulted with astrologers. The Roman emperors were particularly notorious for consulting astrologers, but it was nearly always in their own interest. If they had an astrologer 'prove' they were destined to be emperor or that the action they were carrying out was the right one, then all the better. They weren't so interested in using astrology to understand themselves or the world around them, just on how it could be used to further progress their ambitions. Other leaders who have consulted astrologers also include Queen Elizabeth I and, strangely or perhaps not, Ronald Reagan. It is said that the more dubious aspect of astrology—daily horoscopes—regained popularity after a British newspaper printed a novelty item for the birth of Princess Margaret, printing her horoscope and making claims about what the stars had in store for her.

Now, in this day and age, with the internet, podcasts, and apps, and a world of uncertainty and fake news where the accepted ways of the world are no longer trusted, astrology is going through yet another rebirth, particularly for 'millennials,' it seems. There is an app called Bull and Moon which helps people decide on the stocks they want to buy according to their zodiac signs. A site called Sanctuary will give you a fifteen minute text message reading (for a price, of course) (Judkis, 2019). The many memes that now crop up about astrology are also poking fun at it as well as endorsing it. It wasn't helped when one of the astrology apps, Co-Star, hit the headlines due to some of the strange messages it was sending to its followers, presumably a fault of its AI software. Suggestions included to "fake laugh" your way through the day and to wrap a love letter round a brick and throw it through the window of the person you desired (Pochin, 2019). Some pointed out maybe this was just a clever marketing ploy to grab people's attention, which if so, it did the trick. Whether anyone would have signed up to their app as a result, though, I am not so sure.

The Chinese and East Asian forms of astrology are perhaps the most famous of alternatives to Western astrology. They use 12 animals to define characteristics of 12 different types of personality. They are based on a cycle of years and lunar months, which begins with the Rat and ends with the Pig (not that it actually ends as it is a cycle). We are in the year of the Rat at the moment, which means we have come to the beginning of the cycle once again. One good thing about having an animal each year is that if you know your Chinese zodiac, you've got a good chance of being able to work out someone's age by asking what sign they are. The myth that has grown up around these 12 is that, in fact, there was a race between animals and the first 12 finishers were the 12 animals making up the zodiac ("The Chinese Zodiac," 2020). The goat is considered the unluckiest zodiac sign and end up followers rather than leaders, while dragons are considered the best sign and the ones that make the best leaders. My wife is the sign of the dragon, and I usually end up doing what she says, so that one could be true! The use of astrology in China remains widespread and is mainly used for the big events in a person's life—birth, marriage (and who you are compatible with) and death (your burial must be on a 'good' day). There are also copies or slightly different versions of this zodiac in Korea, Vietnam, Japan and Thailand.

India is another country where the use of astrology remains widespread, and it is considered one of the oldest versions of astrology. In 2011, the Bombay High Court rejected a motion that challenged astrology as a science (Vyas, 2011). Since the earth moves on its axis, there are claims that Indian astrology has a better chance of being more accurate because it follows the sidereal (equatorial) zodiac system, which means it changes every 72 years, rather than the Western tropical zodiac system, which never changes and so, by that logic, is only becoming increasingly inaccurate.

The sheer cultural impact to the world from astrology is easy to see. Words such as 'influenza' and 'disaster' derive their meanings from believed celestial impacts (Influence, n.d.; Disaster, n.d.). The New Age Movement that started off in the 1960s was referred to as the "Age of Aquarius," which referenced the moving of the sun into the sign of Aquarius after two thousand years, and had its cultural impact increased in that well-known tune from the *Hair* musical.

Also, consider "Dark Side of the Moon" by Pink Floyd, a seminal musical work of the 197os, which has among its songs the study of madness—the word 'lunatic' of course coming from lunar and the moon—and thinks about the impact the moon can have on a person's character and well-being. Of course, our body is 75 percent made up of water, and so is it possible that the moon has a direct impact on us, the way that it does on the earth's waves? This is where werewolf stories originate from, strange behaviors around the full moon, but there is no concrete scientific evidence that human behavior does change for the worse around a full moon. Another tune that shows its astrological influences on its sleeve is "No Matter What Sign You Are" by Diana Ross and the Supremes, which follows some of the advice I am going to give in chapter 3 on dating.

There are plenty of other words that take their meaning from the ability for the celestial bodies to influence our behavior and characteristics demonstrating the cultural influence astrology has had over the years. Something like the phrase "born under a bad sign" which became a blues song, and in turn influenced the song "Woke Up This Morning" by Alabama 3, which became the opening theme for one of the greatest T.V. programmes of all time—*The Sopranos*. Using that song as the theme was a stroke of genius as it gave a feeling to the viewer that the only reason Tony Soprano ended up as the main Mafia man and ended up in many of the situations that he did, was due to being "born under a bad sign." If only he had been a different star sign, maybe his life would have turned out completely differently. Although the truth is, if you are born into the Mafia, I can't imagine there are too many ways to get out of that situation, alive anyway. Once you have read chapter 2, which explains the star signs, I don't think it will come to you as any surprise that Tony Soprano is a Leo. So, my personal view is he was going to end up as head of the Mafia. He definitely was born to be a leader of some kind, that much is for sure.

Many writers took 'inspiration' from astrology as well. Both Shakespeare and Geoffrey Chaucer mention astrology within their works, and more 'modern' thinkers such as Carl Jung found a usefulness in studying astrology, even if they did not take to it wholeheartedly.

So, who are the great astrologers of all time? It is claimed that the three wise men mentioned in the bible were, in fact, astrologers (Fonseca, 2020). It would explain why they were looking up at the stars that night and saw the significance in the star they followed. Given they were only mentioned in the gospel of Matthew and so little is written about them, it can only be conjecture. Of course, Nostradamus is always held up as an example. It is claimed he predicted the Second World War, the assassination of John F. Kennedy, and many an apocalypse. Personally, I think his genius was in writing things that were both completely vague and yet full of detail, so that anyone could find what they were looking for within his writing if they wanted to. If he could really predict the future, he would have written it in a clear and plain language.

William Lilly was a famous English astrologer of the 17th century who was brought before the committee investigating the 1666 Great Fire of London, because it was believed he had predicted it many years previously with an image of a city in flames surrounded by coffins (Lily, 1681). I'm not sure it took much imagination to imagine a city of wood burning down, but there we go—who am I to argue with an apparent genius?

Alan Leo is another English astrologer, and he is considered the man that made astrology 'popular' again after its initial decline during the 18th century. He took his last name from his star sign. He was a Leo. It is he who really made strides in terms of not trying to predict world events through astrology, but concentrating on the effect on the star signs' personalities and characteristics. An influence on this may well have been because in 1914 Leo was prosecuted for unlawfully pretending to tell fortunes. The charges were dismissed, but Leo gave a warning to his fellow astrologers to move away from the Nostradamus type of astrologer that had previously been the norm. However, he was prosecuted again in 1917 and this time lost, having to pay a five-pound fine plus legal costs. He died not long after trying to recover from the stress of the trial (Bessie & Besant, 1919).

There are plenty of astrologers making their fame and fortune today, though some of them usually do it with a twist. One of the most popular internet astrologers is Chani Nicholas, who doesn't just give the usual suggestions and predictions, but usually has a strong social justice message to go along with it. In these times of Black Lives Matter protests and a pandemic where the poor tend to suffer most, that's probably what the world really needs right now. Personally, I would say there isn't a particular need to follow an astrologer, other than for entertainment value. They don't know you, so they can't really help you unless what they are saying happens to coincide with what you are thinking. I don't either, but through this book I am going to give you the understanding and tools you need to be able to apply astrology for yourself. You can be your own astrologer. You can understand why you are the way you are, your purpose in life, how you relate to everyone else, and the world around you. You don't need to pay anyone else to do it; you can learn it for yourself. Once you understand the secret language of astrology, you can be fluent in how to make your life better.

Once upon a time, astrology in Western Europe was considered a scholarly pursuit. Those days are long gone, and science has rejected astrology, quite rightly. St. Augustine's observation that if twins born on the same day can have completely different personalities and have completely different things happen to them, this demonstrates the ineffectiveness of astrology, still holds true (Hess & Allen, 2017) That hasn't stopped one of the modern astrology pairings, the "Astro Twins," from having a successful astrology career!

It is not just science that has rejected astrology. As the previous mention of St. Augustine makes clear, the Catholic Church was and is very much against astrology and the use of horoscopes—although a look into the history of some of the Catholic church suggests that wasn't always the case. A lot of the Popes of the Middle Ages were into astrology big time, and it is said that prior to laying the cornerstone of the St. Peter's Basilica, Julius II consulted a horoscope before deciding the best time to lay down the stone (Manning, 2015).

If you are a Catholic reading this and worried you are committing a sin, I would say it is one thing to read and deeply believe your daily horoscope, but quite another to take an interest in the skies above you and wonder how they can help you be the best person you can be. Astrology is not a science, but it can be used as a helpful guide to understanding you and understanding the world around you. There's a reason people have been looking up at the skies for all these thousands of years, trying to work out what our place is in the world, what our place is in the universe. Astrology can be a really useful way of asking those questions and finding things out about yourself and working out what it is you want to do with your life. Just don't start to refuse a job offer because one planet or another is not in alignment with your star sign. Refuse it because you don't want to do it or it doesn't suit you!

The truth is that even with the assistance of astrology, the only way you ever learn is by making mistakes. If you have never made any mistakes in your life, chances are you never learned anything. Even with your newfound knowledge of astrology, don't be afraid to make mistakes and get things wrong. It is in the nature of a human being; we have flaws. Astrology might help you embrace your specific flaws, though, rather than reject them. That in it itself is one of many really good reasons why you should take an interest in astrology and keep reading. By the end of this book, you will have a good grip on yourself and those around you, and be prepared to make a better you and a better life for yourself.

Chapter 2:

What Are Star Signs?

The star signs are meant to represent the 12 constellations that the sun appears to pass through as the earth moves around the sun. The order of those signs are: Aries, Taurus, Gemini, Cancer, Leo, Virgo, Libra, Scorpio, Sagittarius, Capricorn, Aquarius, and Pisces. The characteristics and attributes associated with each sign come from the element they are associated with: fire, water, earth, air, and which celestial body 'rules' their constellation. Let's look at each individual star sign and the characteristics and attributes they are meant to embody:

Aries (March 21—April 20): Aries, represented by the ram, is the first in the cycle. Those that are Aries are often considered to put themselves first. They tend to not have any fear and are usually very driven and willing to get stuck into any situation that would scare off some of the other star signs. A lot of this comes from the fact Aries is a fire sign. Fire signs usually provide leaders. Aries tend to maintain a happy outlook on life, but they can be angered by people who want to delve into the finer detail when there isn't a need to. This tends to spill over into their love life, where they like things to be quick and over with. Aries is ruled by Mars, which is the Roman god of war. Aries can be known for getting very angry without too much of a reason, although they soon calm down.

Taurus (April 20—May 20): Taurus, represented by the bull, is an earth sign. So, as you might expect from someone close to the earth, they often like chilling out in beautiful scenery, close to nature, listening to the birds chirp, smelling the lavender, and eating the sweetest of strawberries. The ruling planet of Taurus is Venus, which is the goddess of love. Taureans loves to be loved, whether that be from people or the finer things in life. Taureans are open to the luxurious and opulent lifestyle. Still, Taureans don't expect this lifestyle to come for free. They know they have to work for it, and they are driven to earning that lifestyle. They have their heads screwed on straight. They are just as capable of saving the money they earn as splurging it on the things they love. Taureans need to feel secure both in their life and in their relationships, and any threat to that security fills them with dread and fear. However, this sometimes works out to their detriment. Hanging onto that security can sometimes mean they stay in things longer than perhaps they should, whether that be a job or a relationship.

Gemini (May 21—June 20): Gemini is known as the celestial twins, and that is often the experience of Geminis—two people. This can mean they may contradict themselves at times, but it does not mean they are fake or hypocrites. They love to learn, and will engage in a variety of hobbies and have many circles of friends. They are social chameleons. They really can fit in anywhere and feel comfortable around anyone, and make other people feel comfortable around them. Geminis tend to be the kind of people who have the latest gadgets or are following the latest trends. However, they quickly move from one to another like a bee going from flower to flower. Gemini is ruled by the planet Mercury, which is a god of messages amongst other things, hence Gemini's love of social situations and talking to people.

Cancer (June 21—July 22): Cancer, represented by the crab, is a water sign. Cancers tend to have great instincts; they can trust their gut. Like a crab in its shell, they can also be very protective and want to safeguard all situations. Also like the crab shell, they can have cold exteriors, but if you take the time to get to know a Cancer, you will find the inside is much softer and kinder. Cancers tend to be happiest at home. They like to truly make their house a home with family and friends. They are always looking after or out for somebody or other, which can be a problem if they go from looking after to actually dictating to the person what they should or shouldn't be doing.

Leo (July 23—August 22): Leo is represented by a lion, and if you are following the gist of star signs, you won't be surprised to learn it is a fire sign. It's no coincidence that a lot of famous Leos are actors and singers, because Leos love the applause of the crowd and love to be in the spotlight celebrating what they have achieved. As a fire sign, they have leadership pretensions. Leos tend to get themselves into those kinds of relationships where they are forever breaking up and getting back together. They love nothing better than a melodrama, hence they are drawn to artistic pursuits. Leo is ruled by the sun, hence their wish to bask in the light. Although the above point suggests they are not great in relationships, actually, like a lion in its pride, they are usually loyal and committed. The only issue becomes if their partner starts to outshine them and their ego gets hurt and bruised; then their loyalty will come into question. Leos are known for their courageous attitude, which again may be why they get drawn to the arts. The reward of success far outweighs the fear of failure for them.

Virgo (August 23—September 22): Virgo is represented by the goddess of agriculture and is an earth sign, perhaps showing its down-to-earth and deep-rooted attitude. They tend to listen to reason, so if you need to persuade them of something, persuade them with logic. It is said that Virgos are perfectionists, but as a Virgo myself, I believe this is misinterpreted. It is more that Virgos like things to be right, not perfect, and if that rightness is disrupted, they can feel all at sea. It means Virgos are quite principled as well, but only up to a point. Their grounded nature means they are more than capable of being pragmatic when it is truly required. Virgos tend to be very conscientious and have great attention to detail, and they are happy following a routine. Like Gemini, Virgo is ruled by the planet Mercury, the god of messages, but unlike Gemini, this does not result in being happy in social situations and talking to all and sundry. Instead, the Virgo internalizes all their communication, and the best way they will express themselves is actually through other forms such as writing, music, and art, not conversation. However, that makes Virgos excellent listeners. If ever you need to talk through a problem or just vent for some time without being harshly judged, the Virgo is the best person to speak to. They will soak up all the information you are telling them and, because they have genuinely listened to you, probably give you some good advice if they are feeling brave enough to engage in two-way communication. This ability to be able to soak up information and have attention to detail also makes them great speed readers or minute-takers. Virgos tend to make very loyal friends, colleagues, and spouses, and are supportive in their own quiet way. They are usually kind and gentle souls deep inside, though getting them to open up that side of them to you is a very great challenge.

Libra (September 23—October 23): Libra is represented by the scales and is an air sign. Like those scales, Libras are on a quest to find the right balance in their life, and if that balance is tipped one way or another, they can become discombobulated. Libras are ruled by the planet Venus, and so, rather like Taureans, Libras like the finer things in life and aspire after sophistication. The balance that Libras seek means they are often very good in relationships, always seeking to get the balance right and perfectly offset their partner. Of course, if their partner is aesthetically appealing, that will always help to make up the mind of the Libra as to whether they want to be with that person or not. However, always seeking that balance means Libras can often try to end up pleasing just about everybody—partners, friends, family, colleagues—and, of course, end up pleasing nobody. Some partners might be left questioning where Libra's loyalties really lie. Being a sign that likes to please people means they are very good in social situations, happily chatting away to people and telling them what they want to hear.

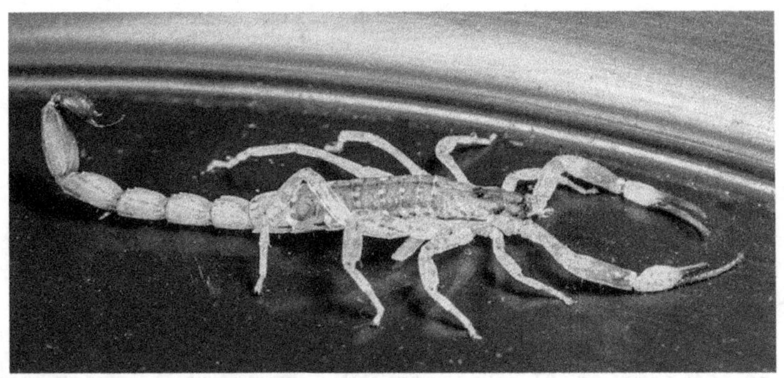

Scorpio (October 23—November 21): The Scorpio is represented by the scorpion and is a water sign. Like other water signs, Scorpios can usually rely on their gut instincts and have an almost otherworldly ability to know what is going on. Scorpios are very much strategists; they plot their moves well in advance. You're going for a promotion, you think you've got a good chance, and yet someone else gets it. You didn't even know they were interested in the role. Yes, that was probably a Scorpio that overtook you, and they started thinking about how they could get that role long before it was even advertised. The closed nature of the Scorpio and their idiosyncratic ways are what make them so beguiling to the other star signs. Scorpios are the kind of person you fall in love with and you are not even sure why. Scorpio is governed by the planet Pluto (or is it a planet? Discussions continue to this day). Pluto being the god of both the underworld and wealth shows the differing natures that you might get from a Scorpio. Definitely capable of harmful and toxic behavior, they are also very good at achieving what they set out to do and building something from nothing. If you can get a Scorpio to trust you, then you will see the best side of them and you may well be able to profit from it.

Sagittarius (November 22—December 21): Sagittarius is represented by the archer and is a fire sign. So, you know what this means? Yes, they have leadership qualities. They are also very curious and adventurous, so you may well find yourself following one to the North Pole on some kind of expedition, or up Mount Everest, or maybe just on a very exotic holiday. Jupiter is the planet that dominates Sagittarius, and as Jupiter was the Roman god of the sky and thunder, that explains that need to traverse the world on daring travels. Due to such traveling, they are world-wise and are known for their sense of humor and for holding court at parties with their tall tales. However, they have to be careful not to go too far and come across as know-it-alls or the kind of person that is constantly one-upping everybody. Just because they enjoy traveling doesn't mean they want to do that alone. They are perfectly compatible and are happy to go on their adventures with a partner. Just be prepared to expect the unexpected if you get together with a Saggitarius.

Capricorn (December 22—January 19): Capricorn is an earth sign and is represented by the sea goat. Until I studied astrology, I had never heard of them, and that is perhaps because it is a mythical creature and not one you are likely to bump into down your local park. It apparently has the body of a goat with the tail of a fish. I'm not quite sure what the point of such a creature would be, but who am I to argue with those that invent mythical beings? Capricorns are usually very steadfast and not easily put out of their stride or off course. However, this incredible focus they have can seem to others as being quite cold and abrasive at times, and not capable of displaying their emotions. Capricorn is ruled by the planet Saturn, god of many things, including periodic renewal, something Capricorns know all too well as they try to make their way through life and navigate the various milestones of life. Strangely though, despite this, it is suggested that Capricorns very rarely look their age and always appear younger than their years— annoying in teenage years, but very advantageous in later life. Capricorns tend to appear reserved to begin with, but get a drink or two in them and suddenly they are the life and soul of the party! Capricorns have a very positive attitude to tasks. If you need someone to do something others might be put off from, Capricorns are your people. This can often translate into being good leaders as well. However, sometimes they can't switch off if they still haven't completed their tasks, and they do sometimes have the tendency to treat their loved ones more like their employees at times.

Aquarius (January 20—February 18): Aquarius is an air sign and is represented, not by the group who sang "Barbie Girl," but by the water bearer. Perhaps not surprisingly, the Aquarius can quite often be an environmentalist or someone who is concerned about the people in war-torn countries or places of famine. They are perhaps the most democratic of the star signs, believing that power should lie at the bottom of the pyramid and not at the top. They are not really ones for authoritarian dictatorships; Aquarians cannot help but rebel and do the opposite of what an authority wants. Aquarians really do follow their own path; they are completely unique individuals with their own style and ways of doing things. Aquarius is ruled by the planet Uranus, god of the sky, which perhaps is why Aquarians are so free-spirited. Aquarians do have a tendency to get a bit carried away with sorting out the world, which can lead to the breakdown of relationships with partners, friends, and family, as their crusade to resolve the world's issues neglects their attention to their everyday life. Due to this, Aquarians can be seen as a bit long in the tooth and bullheaded. Therefore, Aquarians do not like to be dictated to or controlled. They need to find things out for themselves, and if you find yourself with an Aquarian, it is best not to try to immediately rein them in too much as you are likely to rub them the wrong way. If you gain their trust, they might be more susceptible to any constructive criticism you may want to pass onto them.

Pisces (February 19—March 20): Pisces is a water sign and is represented by two fish. Pisces tend to be the most understanding of others out of all of the star signs, capable of showing empathy and sympathy to others and generally having a caring nature. However, this can lead to being oversensitive and becoming swamped by their emotions, believing the world is against them when it is not, or being hurt by things that any other star sign would not spend a second worrying about. Pisces is ruled by the planet Neptune, god of the sea. Although Pisces can leverage all the power and magnificence of the sea, they also bear the danger of swimming out of their depths and needing to be rescued by emergency services. Pisces can often be prone to bouts of nostalgia, speaking about the "good old days," and giving people a chance when perhaps they would be best keeping them at arm's length. But, because of this unassuming nature, they are kind and gentle people, and anyone who gets to know a Pisces will be wowed by their impressive intuitiveness and ability to put themselves in your shoes.

So, you can see how once you start looking at the star signs characteristics using also the element it relates to and its ruling celestial body, you can begin to build up a picture for people born under that star sign. Of course, it should not all be taken as the gospel truth. Generalizing characteristics for all people born during a certain period of time is always going to be hazardous. It is almost inevitable that if you look at the characteristics of your star sign, there may be some you agree with and some you don't.

Having said that, I think sometimes the characteristics get misinterpreted, as with my example for Virgos. I don't know any Virgos that I would describe as perfectionists, but all the Virgos I know, including myself, do like certain things to be right and proper. When they are not, they get a bit more flustered than a person normally would.

Also, as has been pointed out with the controversy over whether a thirteenth constellation should be included, the earth wobbles on its axis, and so where your constellation was when these star signs were first created is not where the constellations are now. Therefore, are you really the star sign you think you are? Astrologers tend to say it doesn't really matter. 12 constellations were picked as it nicely fits in the way we measure time, and there isn't going to be a huge difference in terms of movement, so chances are your star sign is still the same. Nevertheless, as astrology is not an exact science, or a science at all, I think it is useful to pay attention to the star sign before and after your own, as you may find you have attributes from all three that actually make up your own personality. My wife is an Aquarius, but I see traces of both Capricorn, the sign before, and Pisces, the sign after, in her. Perhaps because astrology is not an exact science, and no one has made any changes to the dates and constellations since they were first formed, people can have attributes that overlap more than one star sign in a row.

Taking all that into account, though, you can see how once you have a picture of the kind of characteristics and attributes your star sign has, you can use that to start to make the best of your life. What work could you possibly look into that you hadn't thought of before? There may be hobbies you always felt like you had an interest in but weren't brave enough to pursue. Now you can see from your star sign that your instincts were right and you should be taking that hobby up. You can see the kind of partners you should be avoiding. If you are an Aries and you are with someone who wants to keep discussing the most minute of details even though it is not necessary to do so, they are probably driving you mad. Perhaps this isn't the relationship for you. Or you always wondered why that family member always wound you up more than anyone else, and now you realize it is because they bear a trait that your star sign just can't stand.

As with life, the attributes you have can also dictate issues you may have with your health, or get you to be wary of the kinds of health issues you may have if you don't look after yourself. To bring us right up to date, it can also have a bearing on how you may have been coping with lockdown and the pandemic and may explain why some star signs may be dealing with the world today a lot better than others. Let's take the knowledge you have found in this chapter and start to apply it to the various areas in your life so that you start to think about improving you and your life. You are starting to pick up a few words of astrology and starting to be able to hold a conversation. Now it's time to become fluent!

Chapter 3:

Dating

One area where knowing the behaviors and attributes of your own star sign and other people's star signs can be very useful is dating. This can be if you are in a relationship and you can't work out why it's not working out, or you are in a very successful relationship and it feels like you lucked out and you don't understand why it works as well as it does. Studying star signs and their relative qualities and flaws can really help with answering these types of thoughts. For the purposes of this chapter, I am only going to talk about dating, but from the information I am going to pass on, those in negative or positive relationships can use it to understand why things might work or not work in their relationships. One thing to say straight off the bat, which is a recurring theme, is that astrology is not a science, and so all of this is not to be taken literally. If you're on a date and it's going really well, but you ask the person their star sign and it's one you are not usually compatible with, don't just write them off and think it'll never work out. There are always exceptions to rules, and as I have advised in the previous chapter, sometimes people can be a mixture of their own star sign and the ones previous to and after their own. Sometimes people only have a couple of the attributes associated with their star sign, so they may not have all the flaws that go with that star sign. Always keep an open mind. This is just a guide and no more than that; you never know when the right one for you might appear.

A lot of astrologers take the route that most star signs within each element are good matches for each other: fire signs with fire signs, water signs with water signs, etc. While there may be some truth in that—after all, the star signs within each element stand a better chance of understanding each other—I'm not sure it is necessarily best that you try to search for a sign within your element. I personally find that approach a little too simplistic; life is not as simple as that. After all, most fire signs demonstrate some kind of leadership qualities. If you put both of them together, they may well end up butting heads no matter how much they may understand each other. So, although you shouldn't rule out dating someone from within your element, don't be too scared to look outside your element as well. The other easy option for astrologers to suggest is to go for somebody who is in a star sign that is six months from your own star sign and so is considered an opposite to you. This can be a bit of a risk, as sometimes being opposites can cause a world of pain as you are never able to understand each other and everything you do rubs the other person the wrong way. But, sometimes, there really is some truth in the old adage that "opposites attract." If it was good enough for Paula Abdul to sing about, there must be something in it—though from what I recall of the video, she seemed to be matched with a cat, so perhaps it's best not to follow her advice! Anyway, sometimes being opposites mean you complement each other. Your strengths are the other person's weakness and vice versa, and this means as a team you are unbeatable.

In terms of star signs to avoid, one easy way to work this out is to count two star signs either way away from your own. It is believed dating a sign two away from your own is likely to end up in arguments and a failure to express yourself correctly or easily. (Faragher & Saint-Thomas, 2020). Again, don't rule anything out. There are always exceptions to rules, but I think there probably is something in this. Those star signs are a little close to your own for comfort, and chances are, they won't complement you, they will just rub up against you. I also personally believe dating someone who is the same star sign as you is unwise. There are exceptions—I know of one happily married couple who are both Virgos—but I think it has more to do with them both being easy-going, happy-go-lucky people than it does with both of them being Virgos. Generally, you don't want someone who is the same as you; otherwise, you both have the same weaknesses and working together as a team becomes nearly impossible. People who are in the same star sign as you do make very good friends and acquaintances, because they will understand at least a small part of you and will be able to empathize and sympathize with you most of the time. So, here we go, sign by sign. Let's see which star signs tend to match up best:

Aries: Arieans are considered a bit of a force of nature, and so it is not any old star sign that can cope with them and their irascible ways. Most astrologers will suggest fellow fire signs Leo and Sagittarius are good for Aries as they are a match for them, and will be impressed by their ways rather than put off. There is some truth in that, but I prefer to go for signs that are different enough to compliment Arieans' nature to still be impressed by their ways and personality, but are also different enough to tell them when they are making a bad impression rather than a good one, and show them a way that things can be done differently, and therefore help the Ariean grow as a person. That sign is quite possibly a Libra. As you may recall from the previous chapter, it is the Libra who seeks harmony and balance in life, and so they may well just be able to get the Arieans to do the same and strike up the perfect partnership with them.

The signs that are considered more reactionary and not so open to change are the ones for Aries to steer clear of. These include Cancer and Capricorn, who just won't be able to cope with the impulsiveness and impetuousness of an Aries. Equally, Aries will become quickly bored by these signs' wish to delve into the minutest details when planning things and discussing things. However, if these signs get together and work at it, they will find their differences are the other's strengths, and if they can be humble enough, they will learn a great deal off of each other. Unfortunately, Arieans are not known for their humble qualities.....

Taurus: Virgos and Capricorns are usually good matches for Taureans, as they very much admire the Taurean's love of the finer things in life. It is not an inherent feature of those signs' personalities, and so they really respect Taureans where other signs may be less impressed. In terms of opposite signs, Scorpios can be a good match for Taureans. Scorpios are very good at playing the long game and can be a good complement to the hard-working nature of the Taurean, helping them to build the wealth that could let them keep enjoying those things of comfort that Taureans so enjoy. Of course, Scorpios can have that toxic side of them, so it is a risk for a Taurean, but definitely an interesting one, and if it works out, one that could pay off handsomely.

Taurus is, as we know, represented by the bull, and so Taureans have that reputation for being 'bull-headed' and not easily giving in or compromising. Therefore, other signs that stand a good chance of demonstrating that behavior are usually best left alone. Aquarians and Leos are usually not good at compromise either and like to be right. If a Taurean ends up in a relationship with either of these, chances are there are going to be many arguments and lots of sulking and bickering. They say to never go to bed angry; if these signs got together they'd be lucky to ever go to bed without a cross word having been exchanged. That's not to say a match between them is impossible, but they would both really have to focus on compromising and sharing and knowing when to pick a fight in order for the relationship to work.

Gemini: Ah, the celestial twins. And yes, it is true, dating a Gemini can be like dating two people rather than just one! It can be completely mesmerizing and fascinating, but it can also be very frustrating. Due to their social chameleon ways, it can be very tiring being with a Gemini, listening to all that chatting and social interaction, particularly if your instincts are the opposite and you'd rather find a hole to go and hide in. It is said that their fellow air signs Libra and Aquarius really appreciate a Gemini and so make a good match. That may be a bit simplistic, particularly for an Aquarian. Sure, they are both sociable, but they may both want to be the center of attention at times, and so whether they can both achieve that is not likely. I would say Aquarius may make for a better friend for Gemini rather than a lover. If the Gemini is to look outside their element, the best match for them well may be the Sagittarius. Sagittarius with their curiosity and adventurousness are likely to find the Gemini of great interest and be only too happy to take part in the constant social experiment that being around a Gemini feels like. The only danger may be that, being a fire sign, a Sagittarius may be inclined to try to take over, and if they start dictating to the Gemini, things could get a little heated. As long as they can rein that aspect of their personality in a bit, then Gemini and Sagittarius really could be a match made in heaven.

It's not too hard to work out which signs are the ones to avoid for a Gemini. It's the signs that are not so sociable and are more introspective, like the Virgo or Pisces. Trying to make them constantly have a conversation or taking them to places where they have to talk to a lot of people is just going to depress them. They would rather be alone reading a book or something, not having to talk to strangers all the time. Having said that, as long as Gemini is aware of this and is empathetic to the ways of the Virgo and Pisces, then the relationship can work, with the Gemini helping to bring Virgo and Pisces out of their shell a little bit and improve their social abilities, and the Virgos and Pisces can help the Gemini slow down a little and take the time to smell the roses. That is in an ideal world, anyway. Realistically, they would probably annoy the hell out of each other!

Cancer: Cancerians normally need a little help opening up, and so their fellow water signs Scorpio and Pisces are considered good matches as they have good instincts and should be able to know when to prise a Cancer crab out of its shell and when not to pry too much. Outside of their own element, it is suggested the best match for a Cancer may well be the Capricorn. As Capricorns are not ones to get blown too easily off course and will remain true to a task until it is done, they may well have the patience and thoughtfulness required to really get the best out of a Cancer, and being a little reserved themselves until you get to know them, Capricorns should be able to understand what is going on inside a Cancerian's head. The only concern might be that as they are both capable of being reserved initially to strangers, they may never reach that point where they get to know each other. If you are a Cancer or Capricorn dating the other, put in that little extra effort to get to know them and gain their trust; it will be worth it in the end.

The signs that Cancerians should keep at arm's length are those that don't appreciate that reserved side of Cancer—namely Aries, who as we know can be very stubborn, doesn't want to get bogged down in detail, and can fly off the handle at the drop of a hat. This is not a good match for Cancer unless Aries can tone that side of them down dramatically, and Cancer can be a lot more open and upfront at the outset. Libra is also considered a bad match for Cancer. Their people-pleasing habits may make Cancer uncomfortable, and the people-pleasing may also cover up some of the faults that exist in their partner and in their relationship, and Cancer is not going to be one to confront them about it, so it has the recipe for quite an unhealthy relationship. If Libra can enhance their harmonious aspect and tone down the people-pleasing, then there is hope, but generally, Libra and Cancer are not seen as a good match.

Leo: Leos with their "look at me" attitude, always wanting to be in the spotlight, always wanting everyone's attention—who on earth could be a good match for them? It is suggested that fellow fire signs Aries and Saggitarius are good matches, perhaps because they are the only ones that can understand the drive and desires of a sign like Leo. Personally, I feel like they end up competing with Leo, particularly Aries, rather than complementing Leo. When Leo is around, the other will often have to fade into the background, and I am not sure fire signs are really prepared to do that as often as it would be required. Sagittarius is probably a better bet out of the two. At least they don't like to do things alone even if they do like to take the lead, and they are likely to be a bit more understanding of the Leo's need for attention. They will be a bit quicker to compromise and work as a team with the Leo rather than against them. Outside of their element, Aquarius is considered a good match; certainly they have a big enough personality themselves to cope with Leo's dominant ways. I would still be slightly concerned they may want to compete with the Leo for the limelight, but they have the social skills to cope and will respect and admire the Leo rather than belittle them. If the Leo can find just the right Aquarius for them, then yes, it really could be a perfect partnership.

Leos are best to be very wary of both Taurus and Scorpio. Taurus, with its bull-headed, stubborn ways, is likely to become resentful of Leo's limelight-seeking, and Leo will get frustrated and fed up with Taurus not giving in and never admitting they are wrong. Leos will have no time for Scorpio's game-playing, and Scorpios can have a real tendency to snap sometimes, and with Leos that tendency is likely to come out far more than with other signs. As always, if the signs can rein in their worst flaws, a match between them is not impossible, but the rates of success are low.

Virgo: Wouldn't you know it, but many astrologers suggest fellow earth signs Taurus and Capricorn are best suited for Virgos? On this one, they may be right. One of the reasons they are earth signs is because of how well-rounded and down to earth they are capable of being, so they do suit each other's company well. Taurus is stubborn, but a Virgo doesn't like conflict and is usually willing to compromise and be pragmatic, perhaps after some minimal sulking. So, the two are likely to rub along well together and never quite reach the point of annoying each other. Capricorns are also down to earth enough to bond well with a Virgo. Although they can be reserved, with enough encouragement they can be the life and soul of any situation. They will be able to counterbalance a Virgo's introspectiveness, but at the same time be wise enough not to bully a Virgo into any social situations they are uncomfortable with. Capricorns don't get easily blown off course or put off, so they will also have the patience required to deal with a Virgo who is unable to tell you to your face they love you, but could write you a thousand poems detailing their undying love for you. Outside of the earth signs, a Pisces is considered a good match for Virgos. They are very understanding and empathetic, so, again, will have the required patience to deal with a Virgo's non-sociable preferences. Through gaining their trust, they are likely to have some success in getting a Virgo to be able to open up and maybe even express some kind of emotion without having to write it down or express it through a painting. The only issue is sometimes Virgo do need a push to go and be sociable; otherwise they can end up with too much alone time and start to forget what it is to be a human being. Pisces being as kind and understanding as they are, they might not be brave enough to give Virgo that push. That is why, sometimes, the "opposites attract" theory really does work for a Virgo. Those fire signs that want the spotlight and want to lead might actually find the perfect match in a Virgo who is happy to stay in the shadows and appreciate the greatness of their partner. It is a risk—get a fire sign who bullies and puts down a Virgo and it will be a disaster, but as long as you get a Virgo who is comfortable enough in their own skin and a fire sign who is at least slightly aware of their partner's wants and needs, and it could be a really special and unique partnership. A possible good example of this, although only time will tell, are Prince Harry and Meghan Markle. Harry is a Virgo—although let's be honest, he is not just any Virgo. He is a Virgo who has the confidence of a prince. Still, in my mind this match would not be a good one, and it may explain why, as a couple, they seem to be both looking for privacy and peace and quiet and yet, when it suits them, seeking out the limelight and spotlight in order to express themselves. But they make it work—signs you might not put together, but combine them together and it actually seems to work. They are a very united couple who seemingly support each other in what they want to do. That is why 'opposites' sometimes work.

As alluded to above, signs that Virgos should be wary of are the ones that aren't going to understand the introspectiveness of a Virgo, and rather than encourage them to be a bit more open and sociable, are going to bully them or try to force them into those situations. Anyone that does that will scare a Virgo half to death, and any progress they may have made in getting a Virgo to open up will have been lost, probably for good. Geminis, with their love of a social situation, constant chattering, and tendency to be impulsive would not only put off a Virgo, but they would probably actually be quite scared of them and run the proverbial mile away from them. The Gemini would probably be too wrapped up in their own world to even consider that they might have scared someone off. Sagittarius would probably scare the life out of a Virgo as well, with their love of adventure and the outdoors. Tell a Virgo you want to go and climb a mountain and you want to do it now. "Um, no thanks" is probably the reply you will get, and that's if they haven't already run off to hide in the bushes. But get a Virgo who is a bit more social than the traditional one, or get a Gemini or a Sagittarian who are a bit more introspective than most, and there is always a chance the match could work against all the odds.

Libra: Yes, Libras match well with their fellow air signs, Aquarius and Gemini. Aquarius can appreciate Libra's appreciation of the finer things in life, and Geminis are happy to talk to Libra about it until the cows come home. A celebrity example of this match are Kim Kardashian and Kanye West. No surprise to find out Kanye is a Gemini! Of course for Libra, aesthetics are important (hence Kim Kardashian is a Libra!), so they probably place greater emphasis on the looks of their partner than any of the other star signs. Outside of the air signs, Aries can be a good match for Libra. Aries is strong-headed and wilful, while Libra is all about understanding and people-pleasing. Together that can actually be a great match, as they balance each other out quite well, and are likely to be able to find a compromise between the two of them that means both parties are happy.

Cancers and Capricorns are likely to be the stars that are least impressed by Libra's people-pleasing habits, while Libra is probably going to try too hard to get past the exteriors of those signs into their interiors that just annoy them rather than get them to open up. Well, if Libra can be a little more sensitive when prying and Cancers and Capricorns can be a little more forgiving of Libra's wish to appease all and sundry, the match is still a long shot, but it could just work.

Scorpio: Scorpios can be a tricky partner, with that strategic goal-playing and their ability to snap and sneer. But their fellow water signs, Cancer and Pisces, are not put off by this and admire the way the

Scorpio works. Pisces have a kind and understanding personality, although there would be the worry that Scorpio may take advantage of that nature. Cancer will be able to trust their instincts to know what Scorpio is up to and whether it is for good or bad, and they will be reserved enough not to let Scorpio in until they are sure they can be trusted. Outside of the water signs, the Taurus is considered a great match for Scorpio. Although stubborn, the Taurean's blinkered approach actually suits the Scorpio with their tight-lipped strategies, and when they come together it usually causes fireworks, in the good sense. Taureans know that with Scorpio's clever plans, they can gain the security they have always longed for.

Leos and Aquarians are not such fans of Scorpios. They find them to be secretive and not forthcoming, and they don't like it. The feeling is reciprocated; Scorpios don't appreciate the big-mouthed tendencies of Leos and Aquarians that they feel they can't disclose their secret plotting to. If the signs can be a little empathetic towards each other, they could actually have a very beneficial relationship, but sadly, they usually end up extremely suspicious and wary of each other.

Sagittarius: Of course, their fellow fire signs, Leo and Aqaurius, are considered a good match for the Sagittarians. That could be true, as

Sagittarians like to do things together so they can work well together with others. However, I always think the fire signs end up competing with each other and trying to lead each other, so personally, I think they may annoy each other rather than complement each other. Outside of the fire signs, Gemini are seen as a very good match. Certainly Gemini are happy to talk to Sagittarians about all their adventures and experiences. Whether they would actually take the leap of faith in joining them on that adventure, I am not so sure. Having said that, they often display impulsive behavior without worrying about the consequences, so actually, the two probably do make a great fit. They are both happy to talk about it all afterward as well.

Sagittarians are probably not going to gel well with Virgos and Pisces. See the assessment of the Virgo star sign to see why they would not be a good match. Virgos would probably be scared out of their life with a Sagittarian, and Pisces with their kind nature would probably get completely trampled over by a Sagittarian and end up climbing mountains when they didn't even want to leave the house. Sagittarians would find Virgos' and Pisces' more introspective natures completely frustrating and exhausting.

Capricorn: Yes, you've guessed it, the other earth signs match well with Capricorn. The pragmatic nature of the Virgo would definitely appreciate the dedication of the Capricorn, and the Taurus looks for the kind of security a Capricorn could definitely provide. Outside of their element, Cancer is a good match for Capricorn. Cancers could really see themselves building a home with the focused Capricorn.

Capricorns don't mix so well with Aries and Libras. Aries with their selfish attitude don't appeal to a Capricorn, and Libras with their people-pleasing annoy Capricorns who like to stick to a task and complete it well, even if it might upset someone else. This is a completely different approach to Libra, who will try to do everything for everyone. A match between these types of signs is not impossible, but they both have to bear in mind their more difficult flaws if they want to make the relationship work in the long term.

Aquarius: Aquarians are well-suited to their fellow water air signs, Gemini and Libra. Gemini can chat away with their fellow air sign, support their free-spirited and rebellious nature, and help them in achieving whatever cause they are championing at that time. Libra, seeking harmony in the world and not just in relationships, and who are happy to try to please their partner, are also likely to be very supportive to Aquarians in their various crusades against the world. Outside of their element, Leo is considered a special match for Aquarius. With Leo's leadership and love of the spotlight, and the Aquarian's free-spirited, rebellious ways, if they join together, they really can make a dynamic couple. Of course, such strong personalities mean they may end up clashing rather than combining, but if they can demonstrate the slightest empathy towards each other, they really could take on and take over the world.

Taureans and Scorpios may not be a good partnership with Aquarius. Taurus with its stubbornness and blinkeredness is not likely to put up with the rebellious and free-spirited ways of the Aquarian, and vice versa. Scorpios prefer to take on the world secretly and in private, and without rebelling in such an obvious way. They are likely to look down on the Aquarian's more vocal approach and short-term planning, and Aquarians will get fed up of Scorpio's apparent lack of enthusiasm to join in with their schemes or refusal to share what they are thinking and planning with them.

Pisces: Ah, sweet, kind Pisces. Yes, they get on well with their fellow water signs, Cancer and Scorpio. Scorpio's scheming and smartness is no problem for Pisces; their kindness and understanding will support the Scorpio rather than bring them down, and the Scorpio will appreciate this nature of any Pisces. Cancers couldn't think of anyone better to build a home with than the caring Pisces, and any Pisces would be dreaming of building a home as well, so they would be happy to be with a Cancer and be the one to get inside that shell and bring the true personality of the Cancer out. Outside of their element, Virgos are considered a great match for Pisces. Virgo's practical and introspective nature can actually be a quite good complement to the Pisces' sweet, loving ways. They both appreciate each other and neither tries to force anything on the other, so they would always get along well together and be able to compromise.

Pisces should try to stay away from Gemini and Sagittarius. As seen in the Sagittarius analysis, they would likely trample all over and take advantage of Pisces' kind nature, and it would never be a fair and equal partnership. Gemini's constant talking and impulsiveness is also a turn-off for Pisces, who may be left wondering where the real person begins and ends among all that social behavior.

So, as you can see, when it comes to dating, your star signs and astrology can be very useful in helping you find more out about yourself and why relationships may not be going well for you, and why certain types of people seem to cause the worst experiences for you. But it is just a guide. When all is said and done, every person is unique, and you shouldn't just rule out the chance of a fruitful relationship based on your or their star sign. But it might help you pay a bit more attention to certain sides of your personality and what to be more aware of when you are dating some of the other signs. Good luck!

Chapter 4:

Work

I think we've all been there. You've been given a task to do at work, and the manager wanted it done yesterday. You think, "Why am I doing this? Is this really what I was put on this earth to do?" Well, you're probably doing it to earn money to pay the bills. But, generally, yes, why are you doing that specific job to earn money? Is that really where your skills are best suited? This is where looking at your star sign can really help with working out where your career could be headed and where, if you apply yourself, you could really take off into the stratosphere. Now, as with everything, every person is different. Not every person takes on all the attributes of their star signs, so tread carefully. I don't advise going to your boss tomorrow and resigning just because you read your star sign isn't skilled at booking meetings in Outlook. No, if you want to switch careers or jump jobs, you should plan it very carefully over time. But, using your star sign might just give you that indication as to why you hate your job and why there is another career you've always had your eye on but never been brave enough to go for. Or if you are just starting out on your career path, this is the perfect chance to take stock of what your star sign is or isn't good at and bear that in mind.

Aries: As we know from the previous chapters, Aries like to be first in everything and lead the way. Therefore, they probably need to be in a managerial position where they can tell everybody else what to do, rather than try to take direction from others. They need to be able to delegate. They don't want to be the ones sitting in meetings having to discuss the real nitty-gritty; they just want the info easily presented to them so that they can make the decision. Aries are probably a good sign for being an entrepreneur—the likes of Alan Sugar, Larry Page and Hugh Hefner are examples of entrepreneurial Aries—and starting up their own business. Perhaps they will find an innovative way for a business to run that has yet to be thought of. They are also very driven, so they have the potential to get to the top of their game in a sport as well as in business. Some examples of some top athletes who were born under the sign of Aries are Mo Farah, Linford Christie, and the runner of the first four minute mile, Roger Bannister. Also, the snooker player Ding Junhui, Kelly Holmes, Haile Gebrselassie, Chris Hoy, and the former darts world champion Steve Beaton. To be honest, Aries can probably turn their hand to and make a success of most things, as long as they are the ones doing the telling and not being talked down to.

Taurus: The main thing for Taurus is security, so in the times we are living in, Taureans are probably not having a great time of it at the moment. Taureans are not going to get bored doing a basic nine-to-five job if that is what provides job security. Being stubborn as well, even if you tell them they are in the wrong job, they are not going to listen to you anyway! As Taureans like the finer things in life, perhaps they can find themselves working for a luxury brand or in a hotel that is on the higher end of the spectrum. As they like the outside as well, perhaps landscape gardening is a good choice. Above all else, it's the security of the job that is going to matter to Taureans. So, I have a great deal of sympathy and empathy for Taureans at the moment. Job security is in short supply around the world in most industries at the moment, so it is not an easy time to be a Taurus.

Gemini: Geminis love talking and they love having the latest apps and following the latest trends, so if ever a star sign was born to be a blogger or a YouTube star, it is Gemini. As they are not afraid to talk, anything involving public speaking is good for a Gemini, where it might frighten off any other star sign. It is not impossible to see a Gemini as a university lecturer, or a motivational speaker hired out by companies. Gemini are the least common star sign to have been U.S. president which is perhaps not that surprising, given they can't really concentrate on one thing for too long ("50 Mind-Blowing Horoscope Facts,"Best Life, 2020). Still, you would have thought with all that talking, there might have been a few more of them in the White House over all these years!

Cancer: Cancer's protective nature means they are perfect for working as doctors, nurses, carers, vets, social workers, and any job in those realms where they need to safeguard and take care of people. Cancers also like building a home, so perhaps they can concentrate on jobs where they are building or taking care of other people's homes, such as an architect, estate agent, surveyor, or interior designer. Anything like that is sure to give satisfaction to a Cancer. Maybe even being a bricklayer or being involved in the physical work of building a home would give enjoyment to a Cancer.

Leo: Leos are natural leaders who love the spotlight, so perhaps it is a Leo who is the future president or prime minister of a country. Famous Leo leaders have included Barack Obama, Bill Clinton and Fidel Castro. That love of the spotlight also lends Leos to be actors (Jennifer Lawrence and Daniel Radcliffe for example), and singers (Madonna and Jennifer Lopez, to name but two)—anything where they can get on a stage or get exposure.

Virgo: Ah, yes, our introspective Virgos, who would rather write down what job they want to do rather than tell you. Yes, Virgos are perfect for all those jobs where they need to sit down and think about things rather than constantly talk about them, and with their attention to detail as well, they make excellent analysts, be that business, change, data, finance, and everything in-between. They, of course, make good writers—Stephen King, Agatha Christie, Roald Dahl, H.G. Wells, Mary

Shelley, and Leo Tolstoy are just some of the more famous Virgo authors. They also make excellent copywriters, editors, and secretaries. Being such excellent listeners as well, they can make good counselors and psychiatrists. Virgos tend to like routine, so like the Taurus, they are not against doing the average nine-to-five job, as long as they are getting to use the skills they possess and people aren't putting too much pressure on them to get outside their comfort zone.

Libra: Libras are well-equipped to carry out many roles, and they like pleasing people, so they will always be looking to impress. A Libra would probably make quite a good personal assistant, or an assistant anything, looking to back up and do right by their boss. Just don't expect them to give you that constructive criticism you might need. They are more there to carry out what you want, not tell you when you're making the wrong move. They are associated with scales, which could perhaps extend to the scales of justice, and also for looking for harmony and balance, so they could well make good solicitors and lawyers.

Scorpio: Scorpios being the strategic thinkers that they are, you could place them anywhere where you need them to think out the strategy rather than just get going on something. Technology architecture teams, for example, would be a useful place to have a Scorpio, or perhaps they could be high placed civil servants, helping governments around the world determine the right things to do. Scorpios are actually one of the most common star signs when it comes to the U.S. presidents and world leaders in general, perhaps not much of a surprise given that strategy-driven mind of theirs. Famous Scorpio leaders include Theodore Roosevelt, John Adams, Indira Gandhi, Charles de Gaulle, King William III of England, the Roman emperor Tiberius, Evo Morales, and Tony Abbott.

Sagittarius: As another fire sign, Sagittarians are leaders of people, so they are always useful in managerial positions. Being adventurous and curious, they are definitely suited to being travel agents, pilots, mountaineering guides, or guides for anything dangerous and daring. They will always be excited by jobs where traveling is involved. They are probably sad that that aspect of work is somewhat curtailed at the moment. There are probably Sagittarians around the globe trying to lobby for more testing at airports and less reliance on quarantining people when they arrive in a country.

Capricorn: Being very focused, Capricorns could easily fill top managerial positions or become chairman or chairwoman of the board. Being linked with periodic renewal as well, they tend to be a good fit for insurance agents, tenancy agreement estate agents, or mortgage advisors. Capricorns are also known for maintaining a youthful appearance, so this may well lend itself to a long career as a model or a newsreader, or having some kind of presence in the media. Kate Moss is a Capricorn, for example.

Aquarius: Aquarians lend themselves to helping out with humanitarian causes and nonprofit organizations and charities. Despite being rebels themselves, they are actually very good in management and being chief executives because it is them giving out the orders rather than receiving them. Aquarians do not fare well at the bottom of the pyramid; they will only suffer being at the bottom rung of the ladder if they know they can soon move up. Their free-spirited nature means it is not out of this world for them to pursue something in the arts, such as singing, painting or drama.

Pisces: With their empathetic nature, it goes without saying Pisces can do some of the hardest jobs. They are great counselors, therapists, emergency services, social workers, or anything where you have to show empathy. However, they do have to be very careful to leave work at work and not let their emotions overwhelm them from some of the harrowing things they may have to see and talk about. But they are the sign best placed to help the people going through these things. Strangely enough, Pisces are actually one of the most common star signs to be U.S. president ("50 Mind-Blowing Horoscope Facts," 2020). I can't think of many presidents who had a sweet and caring nature, but there we go. Perhaps things were different once upon a time!

So, you can see that from knowing the attributes and characteristics of a star sign, this can help you to work out where your career may best lie. But every person is unique. Don't turn down a job just because you think it might not suit your star sign. Give something a go. You never know, you may just surprise yourself!

Of course, economic demands mean we don't always get the luxury of picking and choosing what we want to do or who we want to be. Sometimes, we have to do what we have to do just to make sure we can earn some money to pay the bills or look after loved ones. So, don't be disheartened if you are in that situation and you feel you'll never get to do what you are truly meant to do. You are doing the right thing. Hang in there, and hopefully the time will come when you have more financial freedom and you have a chance to reassess where you are in your career. Let's be honest, the job market is a really daunting place at the moment with many countries seeing high unemployment due to the pandemic, and so every job you go for, there are thousands of people also going for that job. Now probably isn't the right time to think about jumping ship or changing careers. If, however, you have been made redundant, and you have the financial security behind you not to have to worry about getting a job straight away, then this might be the opportunity to look at that job you have always wanted to do, and perhaps completing any training and qualifications you might need. Hopefully, if the pandemic eases up in your country, you will be ready to launch yourself into your new career. If you're a recent graduate, you may already have an idea of what you want to do based on how well you seemed suited to the education you have already taken, and, so, while thinking of alternatives is useful, if you really did find you were perfectly suited to the subject you did your degree in, don't ditch it just because it doesn't seem to fit in with your star sign. You know yourself better than any astrologer does.

I have only put some suggestions as to what you might be good at based on your star sign. I'm sure if you let your imagination run free, you can use that logic to think of many other jobs and careers that might be suited to you. It really is a great thing to have the power of knowledge when it comes to star signs and to be able to apply that knowledge to your life. It can make a difference. Just don't take it so seriously that you let it impact your life negatively; just have fun with it. The world of employment is not an easy place to be at the moment, and job security is not easy to come by, but hopefully this chapter has helped you think about what your strengths and weaknesses are and where you might be best placed to find work, keep work, and enjoy your work. If you can enjoy your work and even love your work, that usually adds up to leading a very happy and contented life, and that doesn't necessarily mean having lots of money. Sure, being wealthy is great because it gives you freedom to do whatever you want, but that in and of itself does not necessarily add up to happiness careerwise. The most contentment comes out of your career when you actually enjoy it and love it, regardless of the pay. Of course, if you can get both enjoyment and high pay from your work, then you are living the dream!

Chapter 5:

Hobbies

As with dating and work, so it is with hobbies. Certain characteristics and attributes of star signs lend themselves to certain hobbies. You may have been flummoxed as to why you are so naturally good at something, or you may have always fancied taking up a certain hobby but have just never felt quite confident enough to follow through. If you know the attributes of your star sign and you follow through with the logic, you can know what hobbies you are particularly suited to and you are more likely to have success with and, therefore, enjoy more. Everyone is unique, so not all attributes apply to everyone in that star sign. Just because you are not naturally good at something doesn't mean you should just give up or never take it up in the first place. Sometimes, it is worth putting in that extra effort and time to become competent at something you are not naturally skilled in. But, as a guide, this is useful if you are wondering what you should turn your hand to next or whether the instincts you have been feeling about whether you would be good at something or not are correct.

Aries: Aries like to be out in front and be the first at everything, and they are not easily put off by things that other star signs would run well away from. If you need to find someone to try out the latest extreme sport, Aries are your people. I bet an Aries was the first person to try bungee jumping. Any outdoor sport requiring strenuous physical activity is good for an Aries. Even if they are doing more mundane things like listening to music or watching movies, chances are they have got the volume turned up to eleven and watching that sneak preview or special director's cut that no one has ever seen before.

Taurus: Taureans like the natural things in life, so they will enjoy things like fishing, birdwatching, rambling, hiking, or gardening—anything that gives them the chance to hear the birds and smell the flowers.

Taureans also like the luxuries in life, so if they have built up wealth, they may just want to travel the world staying in and observing all the best things in life. Perhaps one of those really luxurious cruises is something that Taurus has been thinking about and would really enjoy. If so, I am sure Taureans are hoping for a time when the pandemic is much more under control and the thought of going on a cruise doesn't give you palpitations.

Gemini: Gemini is where you get two for the price of one. Therefore, Gemini needs something that engages body and mind, and due to their sociable side, it is probably best they engage in team games. So, any team sports or any sports where you can play doubles will please a Gemini. They love to learn, so taking up further education can be considered a hobby for them, or watching the History Channel, or scanning the World Wide Web for things of interest to them. Geminis love trying out the latest gadgets and trends as well, so you can find them testing out the latest in smartphone or smartwatch technology, or following the latest dance craze, aerobics, or yoga trends with their friends.

Cancer: Cancerians love the home, so they are more than happy getting stuck into all those D.I.Y. tasks lots of normal people hate, tidying up the garden, or just giving the whole house a good spring clean. As they like being at home, they are happy just reading, listening to music, watching the TV, or cooking and bonding with the family while eating their meals. Due to their protective nature they may also enjoy helping out with kids' sports teams or clubs.

Leo: Oh, yes, those Leos that love the spotlight. If they aren't already pursuing it as a career, then they may well be pursuing it as a hobby. Leos are the ones happily volunteering to do karaoke, or getting the lead part in an amateur theater production, or taking up ballroom dancing with an aim to take part in competitions. Anything where they can be the center of attention and outshine those around them is a hobby worth putting time and effort in for a Leo.

Virgo: Virgos tend to be a lot more introspective, and the hobbies on Leo' s list would scare them greatly even if they had skill at them. The Virgo would rather write the lyrics for the singer than sing the songs, or write the play for the actors rather than star in it. Virgos like any activity they can do by themselves—writing, painting, reading. There are any number of activities that Virgo would get a great deal of pleasure from, free from interference from bothersome people.

Libra: Libras are another star sign that do not run away from the opulent lifestyle if they don't have to. So, maybe they can get into luxurious cruising, traveling the world's five-star hotels, eating at fine dining restaurants, going to the opera, or learning to play polo or croquet. As they are also people-pleasers, they can find some of the more artistic endeavors, such as painting, performing music or dramas, very enjoyable, as long as they know there are people watching or partaking that will enjoy their performance. Also, they could get into cooking and let friends and family try their culinary delights. Just don't invite Gordon Ramsey, though. If he gave his usual critique, that would put Libra off ever trying to cook anything again.

Scorpio: With their love of strategic planning, things jigsaws, crossword puzzles, and board games like Monopoly could be of interest to them. Chess or Scrabble are great, too—anything where they have to start thinking about things in advance. They also like building something from scratch so give them some LEGO or Meccano and see what they can make out of it. Or maybe they want to build a shed for the garden.

Scorpios love planning and building, so any hobby along those lines is likely to pique their interest.

Sagittarius: Yep, those Sagittarians seem a bit too daring for many of the other star signs. They love the outdoors and being adventurous. I said it could have been an Aries who did the first bungee jump. Well, maybe it was a Sagittarius instead. You can find them rock climbing, mountaineering, kayaking, whitewater rafting, skiing, or hiking—anything outdoors that requires an adventurous nature, Sagittarians love it.

Capricorn: Capricorns stick to a task and enjoy getting it done, so they are another sign who will probably get on well with the kind of DIY tasks that other signs would find frustrating and end up tearing their hair out over. Capricorns are more than happy to get involved in the practical side of interior and exterior designing.

Aquarius: Being the humanitarians and environmentalists that they are, perhaps if you are an Aquarian, you want to go and join a protest movement, get involved in local politics, help your local church, or get involved in volunteering work. All of those types of things would make an Aquarian happy. With their free-spirited nature, they may find yoga and meditation interesting and may want to find out about different religions and philosophies.

Pisces: Pisces being as sweet and kind as they are, perhaps they want to get involved in volunteering at the local dog or cat home, or a donkey sanctuary. They love nostalgia as well, so perhaps they want to search for those collector vinyl records and hunt down DVDs of the shows they used to love as a kid.

When Is a Good Time to Take On a New Hobby?

In all honesty, any day is a good day. It really doesn't matter. You can always put it to rest and pick it up some other time if it doesn't go that well the first time. But, one way of working out whether a certain time is a good time or not is by working out what the moon is doing. The moon moves from star sign to star sign every two and a half days during its 28-day cycle ("Timing With The Moon In Astrology," 2020) and so this can have an impact on whether things are going to go well or not. According to the moon theory, new activities and hobbies should not be taken up when your star sign is considered "void of course moon" ("Timing With The Moon In Astrology," 2020).

So, what exactly does "void of course moon" mean? Some explanations you see require you go and get a degree in astrology before you stand a chance of understanding it. But, what it means in its basest form is the time before the moon moves into a new sign in which it doesn't really come into contact with any other planets. (Kahn, 2020). So, it can be considered the time the moon goes for a bit of a nap, and all that positive influence it may have had on you is suddenly on the wane. This period is never a time for starting anything new; this period is for completing things or doing really simple tasks that really do not require a lot of brainpower. Doing anything new or taxing in this period is likely to end in disaster.

So, how do you know when the "void of course" timeframe is so you can avoid it? For that, you will need an astrological chart. You can track these down online, or maybe you can speak to a professional astrologer and they will be able to guide you as to when these are. When they strike, avoid starting anything new or making really important decisions. Stick to doing simple things and doing the types of things you have always done without even needing to think about them. The same is true for the previous chapter as well. If you were thinking of changing jobs or starting a new career, the "void moon" is not the time to be doing that. Even interviews can be problematic during this time—though, of course, I urge you not to turn down interviews just because of a "void moon." As advised, things can be challenging during this time, but not impossible, and you should be grateful for and take up any opportunity you can, particularly given the current economic climate following the pandemic. Don't ever let the "void moon" put you off going for an interview or starting a job; just be willing to work and try that extra bit harder to make things work during this period. It doesn't last forever, so be patient and good things will come.

We know to avoid starting hobbies during the "void of course moon" period, but when is a good time to start new things and, therefore, new hobbies? Well, starting something new including a hobby is considered best to do during the 'waxing' period of the moon ('Timing With The Moon In Astrology," 2020). This is the period when the moon goes from a new moon to the full moon. So, generally, the answer is that the time to pick up a new hobby is the new moon. This is when you are going to feel like it's a time for new beginnings and fresh starts, and you aren't just going to give up after the first time of doing something. Your mind is going to be much more open for trying new things during this time. Equally, with the previous chapter, this is time to change jobs or start a new job. Your mind is ready to make that change, so you can go for it. Of course, don't ever only change jobs or start a new job because it is a new moon. Although things tend to be easier during this time for starting new things, never turn down an opportunity if it is something you really want to do outside of this period. It may not come as easily to you outside of a new moon, but you can still make things work by putting in a little extra effort and having a little more patience.

As with "void moons," you can find when new moons are on an astrological chart so you can know the best time for you to pick up that new hobby you always wanted to. Of course, nothing here is definite. Just because things can be more difficult when starting new things during a "void moon" time doesn't mean it is impossible. It might be more challenging but not impossible, and there may even be a lucky few who don't seem to even notice it is a "void moon" time and pick up their hobby with ease, like a swan learning to swim. And just because starting new things tends to be easiest during a new moon phase doesn't mean that is the case for everybody. Maybe you're one of the unlucky ones who starts a new hobby during a new moon phase, finds it impossible, and immediately gives up. Nothing here is predetermined. It is a guide as to when the best time might be, but it is no more than that. Every individual is different, and what may apply to the majority may not apply to you. That also goes for the hobbies themselves. Maybe you are one of those rare people that barely display any of the characteristics of the star sign you were born in and you just don't identify with it at all. Of course, it follows that you probably aren't going to take up any of the suggestions for hobbies any time soon either. We are all different; people within the same star sign are all different, and so you can find your own way and take the advice you find relevant to you. I personally find that for my own star sign, the suggestions are sensible and are things I would enjoy. In fact, I am doing some of those hobbies. But, I knew one person who was a Leo, and you would never have known it. He never sought the limelight. In fact he was a very unassuming person, so the logic for him may not follow through that he should do the hobbies suggested for Leos. Having said that, when he did get up and sing, he did a very good job and enjoyed it, and he was a soccer referee at amateur levels for many years, which is seeking its own kind of limelight, so perhaps the suggestions wouldn't be so wrong after all. Hopefully it will feel right for you, though. Maybe you do identify with your star sign and you now feel more determined to pursue some of these suggestions, or maybe they have come as a complete surprise to you and you are amazed you never thought of them before and want to give them a go. Whatever the situation, have fun, and I hope you take up something that will bring a lifetime of enjoyment to you.

Chapter 6:

Health

First of all, let me make it really clear that if you have any medical issues, concerns, or problems, you should be discussing these with your doctor or visiting a hospital. You should not be discussing them with an astrologist or relying on astrology to tell you the best way to proceed. What astrology can do, though, is make you aware of the kinds of medical problems your star sign might be more likely to suffer from, and then you can guard against and be wary of that. There may even be some behaviors you can stop which may assist with achieving this. If ever you develop any symptoms you are concerned about, though, contact a doctor not an astrologist. Below are the kind of health issues each star sign needs to look out for based on their characteristics.

Aries: The thing that Arians need to watch is their temper. Having a quick temper or getting irritated at seemingly nothing can cause unnecessary stress on the body, and can lead to such things as headaches and migraines. It can even lead to even more serious health conditions, such high blood pressure, a heart attack, or ulcers in the stomach. It is important for Arians to find a way to relax, such as to count to 10 before they blow their top. If Arians can find a way to chill out and relax, they stand a chance of being able to avoid the kind of illness that a lot of their fellow Arians fall foul to.

Taurus: As with Aries, Taurus can sometimes suffer from stress-related illness. This is due to their stubbornness, which can lead to them sulking or feeling angry and holding grudges. This can cause migraines and headaches, and also a pain in the neck. It can in extreme circumstances lead to feelings of depression, which in turn can leave the immune system low and lead to infection and colds. As Taureans are often found wandering about the countryside or taking picnics in fields, they also need to be wary of bites from insects, spiders, mosquitoes, and ticks (depending on where you are in the world). Even if the insect biting you is considered harmless, you can still end up with problems if the bite gets infected. It can even lead to a blood infection, which can be quite nasty. So, Taureans, make sure you find a way to relax, be a bit more forgiving of people and situations, and take care when you are enjoying and appreciating the outside world, and you should be able to avoid the usual health pitfalls that Taureans suffer.

Gemini: Being the social chameleons that they are, Geminis have to be careful with their mental health. They can be prone to bipolar disorder and anxiety. Due to their capacity to talk to everyone and their need to follow the latest fads and trends, when they are left alone it can leave them feeling low and their mind wondering where to turn. Sometimes it turns to some dark places. Geminis really need to make sure they take care of themselves and don't extend themselves too much. The temptation of putting themselves into another social situation they know they will enjoy can be too much, so they need to remember it is okay to say no sometimes. Most importantly, they need to be okay with being alone and being happy in their own company. If Geminis can learn to love themselves as much as they love being sociable, they can avoid the kind of mental health issues many of their fellow Geminis may be suffering.

Cancer: Cancers are known for their hard exterior, and sometimes this means not opening up when expressing their emotions would help them enormously. So, they can end up suffering from stomach ulcers and other stomach issues, and they need to take care of their mental health as well. Otherwise, all that internalizing can end up with someone on the edge of a breakdown if it all gets too much. If a Cancer can just learn to express their emotions a little more and realize it is okay to "let it all out" sometimes, they can avoid the common health problems many of their fellow Cancers may suffer from. Sadly, the terrible disease they share their name from is not something they or any of the other star signs are safe from.

Leo: Leos are definitely a sign that needs to take care of their mental health. With all that seeking the spotlight and craving attention, if the attention isn't there or the spotlight is switched off, Leos can easily end up in a depressed state or with very low self-esteem. Sometimes, they can also seek out melodrama, and that can also cause emotional well-being to take a knock. It can also result in stomach and heart problems or high blood pressure if the stress of those situations gets too much. Leos need to be aware of their worth even when no one is paying attention to them and realize that things don't need to be exciting to be good sometimes. If they can achieve this, they can avoid many of the mental and physical issues their fellow Leos suffer from.

Virgo: With all the introspection, internalizing, and ability to make themselves extremely uncomfortable in social situations or having to do things they don't want to do, Virgos are particularly prone to stomach ulcers and stomach issues. If they put the wrong kind of stress on themselves, they can be prone to high blood pressure, panic attacks, and heart problems as well. Too much introspection can also be a problem mentally; it can lead to depression, particularly in their younger years when they are very emotional but can not find a way to express that through their mouths. Virgos must learn to express their emotions verbally a bit more and not be so afraid of social situations.

They are the opposite of the Gemini, and have to learn that it is okay to say yes sometimes. If they can understand that it can be a good challenge to be outside their comfort zone, then they may avoid the usual health concerns most of their fellow Virgos will encounter.

Libra: As Libras are often on the search for harmony and balance, if any of the star signs are going to be in a good and healthy state, it is going to be a Libra. However, they do have that people-pleasing aspect to their personality, and so they do need to be aware of the mental and physical issues that can sometimes cause. They may well overstretch themselves trying to make everybody happy and end up feeling burnt out or exhausted. There can also be a mental pressure from trying to please everyone. If you don't manage to fulfill that, then it can lead to feelings of depression and/or low self-esteem. Of all the star signs, Libras are likely to be in the best shape, but they do need to take care of themselves and realize they can't please all of the people all of the time. If they can do that, they should be confident of achieving full fitness and a clean bill of health.

Scorpio: Like all the signs, one of the biggest risks for a Scorpio is their mental health. Plotting and planning in secret and being capable of some very toxic behavior can not only have a negative impact on the people around them, but also on the Scorpios themselves. They can be prone to depression and feelings of isolation if things are not going their way, and dishing out toxic behavior can result in toxicity in your own body, which puts you at risk of cancer and other such serious diseases. Scorpios just need to be a bit careful about making sure they express themselves emotionally in a harmonious way and reining in their worst toxic behavior, and remember that showing love to others and themselves is often the best route to a healthy body and mind.

Sagittarius: With all that outdoor adventure, the Sagittarius is at risk of any number of physical injuries, including broken bones, back pain, knee joint issues, or even the possibility of suffering unconsciousness at some point and therefore risking brain injury. Even hypothermia or heat exhaustion and dehydration are possible risks to a Sagittarius. Also, as they love being adventurous outdoors, if they get stuck inside, it is possible they can suffer from claustrophobia. You don't want to get stuck in an elevator with a Sagittarius, unless they work out a way to climb out of the elevator! If Sagittarius can take great care while on their adventures and know their physical limitations, they should avoid some of the physical injuries that come with the territory of being a Sagittarius.

Capricorn: Capricorns may often appear youthful on the outside, but that doesn't mean they are as youthful on the inside. Capricorn's ability to not be put off course (which in unkinder terms may be described as stubbornness), combined with their inability to switch off means Capricorns can be in danger of burnout, exhaustion, and stress. These can lead to stomach and heart issues, high blood pressure and headaches. Capricorns need to be careful and make sure they take the time to take care of themselves and take some time out to relax and find some peace and quiet. If they do that, they should be able to avoid having to see their doctor any time soon for reasons of stress or exhaustion.

Aquarius: Due to their free-spiritedness (which in an unkind way could perhaps be described as clumsiness), Aquarians can often find themselves with bruises, scratches, and blisters. Sometimes, these everyday injuries can cause infection and more serious problems. Aquarians may even suffer severe physical injury if they fall over somewhere or walk straight out into a road. Aquarians just need to be really careful and try to take a bit more care when they are running about saving the world. Sometimes, it is as simple as just looking where you are going. As with a lot of other signs, Aquarians can get a bit carried away with things, so they also need to take the time to take care of their mental health and make sure they are not putting too much pressure and stress on themselves.

Pisces: Pisces can be the biggest danger to themselves. That sweet, caring and empathetic nature of theirs means they are always looking out for others and not themselves. This can leave them tired, burnt out, and exhausted, and make them very prone to picking up colds and other such infectious diseases. Since they are often caring for other people who may be ill, that illness may get passed onto them. Pisces are also prone to become overwhelmed with emotions; this can lead to things like depressions or nervous breakdowns. Pisces are very sensitive as well, so if not careful, they can suffer anxiety, low self-esteem, and insecurity. Pisces need to take as much care of themselves as they take care of others, and must remember to stand strong and not let others take advantage of them. If Pisces takes care of themselves, they stand a good chance of remaining fit and healthy.

It is essential I once again reiterate that if you have any medical issues, problems, and concerns, you speak to a doctor or go to a hospital. They are the ones who will know what is best for you, not astrologers. Don't ever use astrology to decide the best treatment for you or work out what an illness could be. It cannot help you. The other thing to say is that this is just a guide to what the main concerns for each star sign may be. That doesn't mean there isn't a host of illnesses and medical conditions that could potentially befall you. We are all at risk every day we are alive. That has become particularly clear in recent times, so don't take this guide as some sort of confirmation that you are invincible. You are not. There are, sadly, any number of diseases and conditions you could end up with in your lifetime. Hopefully not, but I just want to make sure you don't misinterpret this guide as confirmation you are not going to get cancer or some other life threatening disease. Sadly, none of us are immune from that prospect. We can only hope we are the lucky ones that do not have to go through such things.

Equally, just because I have named certain star signs to be more prone to certain illnesses doesn't mean because you are that star sign you are going to suffer from it. We are all unique and we don't always display all of the characteristics of our star signs, and even if we do, it doesn't follow that that means you will definitely suffer the illnesses those characteristics are more likely to throw up. There are smokers who live well into their hundreds, yet we know that, generally, smoking kills people a lot younger than would normally be the case. We are all unique with different genetics and different metabolisms, so we just don't know what may happen to us in the future healthwise. The best you can do, regardless of your star sign, is try to take care of yourself both physically and mentally.

If I had been writing this many years ago, people would have still been too ashamed and embarrassed to talk about the mental health side of things and wouldn't feel able to open up about things like depression and anxiety. I'm sure a Pisces would tell us it is scary living in the modern world and things were so much better in the old days, but, when it comes to mental health, things are so much better now. Not in terms of the numbers of people suffering from mental health, but that we are now in a world where people can be open about talking about it. Because people are openly talking about it, others suffering know there is nothing to feel ashamed and embarrassed about. As an introspective, internalizing Virgo I know only too well some of the mental health risks that can occur if you are not careful, particularly in younger years. Now that I am older, I seem to be more balanced in my emotions, but when I was younger, my emotions would be up and down and all over the place. I remember often refusing to go out and see my friends and wanting to be alone because I knew I would not be any fun to be around, and if people asked me anything, they were likely to only get a sarcastic or miserable reply back. But, we didn't talk about mental health in those days, so I just suffered without talking about it.

Looking back now and hearing experiences of people who have suffered from mental health issues, I recognize I was probably suffering from depression at the time, and some of my behavior can be recognized in bipolar disorder. I never sought help though, I just suffered. I am just really lucky I made it through without anything truly terrible occurring. Don't rely on luck; make sure you find someone to talk to if you need to. Don't be afraid to talk to people about what you are going through, even if you are a Virgo or a Cancer or anyone else who internalizes rather than externalizes. Don't even hesitate if you're a Leo, because as much as you like the spotlight, I doubt you envisaged the psychiatrist's couch as the place where you would get plenty of attention. So, please take care of yourself, and, hopefully your physical and mental health will be taken care of as a result.

Chapter 7

Coping In a Lockdown

As the previous chapter dealt with illness and mental health, that brings us nicely onto the subject of coping in a lockdown. Wherever you are in the world, you may be in different stages of the pandemic, but chances are you will already have had a lockdown or you are currently in lockdown, or you are concerned there is going to be a second wave and you are getting prepared again for lockdown. Whatever your situation, you are probably wondering why you were so good or bad at coping with that type of scenario. Some people will have felt like climbing up the walls being stuck inside the house for so long, whereas others will have really enjoyed being at home, potentially with peace and quiet, and having to use their imagination in order to get through the day. A lot of this will have to do with what star sign you are, and the characteristics and attributes you have as a result will have determined whether you are good or bad in a lockdown situation. As with all the chapters, I have to point out this is just a guide, you may not have any of the attributes or your star sign or just a few, and so the way I am suggesting your star sign will behave or did behave may not be true for you, or maybe you do have the attributes but you defied the logic and behaved differently than expected. Either way, this is not scientific fact. Equally, the things I suggest your star sign do to help cope with the lockdown may not necessarily apply to you and so it may not make the lockdown any better. This is just a guide of suggestions, not scientific fact. But, based on your star sign, let's see who is likely to cope well with a lockdown and for whom it is their worst nightmare, and for those that cope badly, what they may well be able to do about it to make lockdown a more bearable experience for them.

Aries: Well, Aries does like to be the first at everything, so maybe they entered lockdown before they even officially had to do so. Being fearless and driven, they would have soon become bored and fed up and were probably one of those venturing out when they shouldn't have been. If you were living with an Aries, it could have been quite hard if you attempted to discuss anything in detail with them, and with their ability to get angry quickly, I would have expected there to be some heated arguments. However, the way to get Aries to cope in the lockdown is to give them some very clear goals to achieve each day. If they have that, then that drive that burns inside them is satisfied and they should remain calmer and be less inclined to become irritable. No doubt, though, Aries is one of the signs that would do cartwheels the moment any lifting of the lockdown is announced.

Taurus: On the one hand, Taureans would have hated the lockdown as they love being outdoors enjoying the nature of the world. Having said that, if they are lucky enough to have a garden, then that ability to stay close to nature would not be completely taken away from them. On the other hand, Taureans need security, so they would have felt a lot less secure wandering around with the virus out of control than locked up in their home safe and sound. If they had an appreciative partner living with them, then the need to be loved they have would also be satisfied. So, Taureans are probably coping okay and don't really need to take advice. If you are a partner or a loved one staying with a Taurean, just make sure you give them that love and affection, and they should be able to see through the lockdown just fine.

Gemini: As you can imagine, lockdown is a bit of a nightmare for a Gemini. All those social situations they are usually getting themselves into are cruelly taken away from them. Luckily for them we are living in the 2020 pandemic and not 1918, so although it's not quite the same as being out and about, they are able to swap physical sociability for virtual sociability. In fact, in the virtual world, they may be even more sociable than they were in the physical world. Geminis also love to learn, so this is the perfect opportunity for them to get some online education in and really learn about all those topics they have been meaning to in previous months but just didn't have the time for. So, for Geminis to survive the lockdown, they need to keep their sociability up with video and phone calls to all their circle of friends and family, and make sure they have things to learn and be curious about. Nevertheless, Gemini will be another sign that can't wait for the lockdown to be over so they can get back out there.

Cancer: As we know, Cancers love the home so lockdown is probably quite heavenly to them. If they have a family, they probably love having the family stuck at home with them. Whether the family is as happy is another matter! So, Cancerians are another sign that are probably loving the lockdown and don't really need any advice to get through it. They will be happy looking after people and cooking for people and other such domestic activities.

Leo: Yep, you've guessed it, the lockdown is likely to drive Leos round the bend. They will be going crazy not getting the attention they need, shut away inside away from the spotlight. However, like the Gemini, they can make use of the virtual world out there. They can have video calls with people if they are craving some attention. Leos also like artistic pursuits, so now is the time to make those YouTube videos playing your favorite songs or reading your favorite Shakespeare sonnet or whatever it might be that you wish to show the world. There's no doubt Leo will be another star sign desperate for the lockdown to end, but using the virtual and online world, they should be able to get through lockdown without having a complete breakdown.

Virgo: Virgos, of course, will be happy in the lockdown. They won't mind that their social calendar is reduced to nothing, no high demand for them to have video calls to make up for it, though they will still be happy texting and emailing friends and family. The lockdown gives the Virgo the chance to finally write their novel or finish whatever artistic pursuit they have been meaning to without daily life getting in the way. But Virgos should still make the effort to stay in touch with people; too much time without speaking to people, and the Virgo may be irritable and snappy when lockdown ends and they have to engage in normal daily conversation with people once again. Virgos do like a routine as well, so it is important for them in lockdown to keep that routine. Otherwise, they could find themselves sleeping in and losing a reason to get out of bed, and that way can lie depression. But, generally, Virgos are going to be okay in a lockdown and don't need too much advice to survive it.

Libra: Libras need peace and harmony, so they would probably find the lockdown a bit disconcerting. However, if they have a family, then maintaining the peace and harmony within the family during a lockdown would probably keep them fulfilled. They like pleasing people, so if they can find neighbors or people in their local community that need assistance, this could also help them keep focused and help them not become too dispirited during a lockdown.

Scorpio: Scorpios are probably going to be okay during a lockdown. They like to do all their strategic thinking in secret, so lockdown doesn't impact that. In fact, it makes it easier. The only issue might be that they can plan all they like, but they might not get much of a chance to enact some of those plans. Scorpios are sometimes known for their toxic behavior, so living with a Scorpio during this time might not be so great because they will have no one else to be toxic towards. So, the key to keeping Scorpio happy during the lockdown is to keep their mind engaged. Give them that hope that the lockdown will come to an end and all their planning will have the opportunity to come to fruition, and they should be able to stay positive and keep that toxic behavior to a bare minimum.

Sagittarius: This is another star sign that will not be happy about having to go into lockdown. With all that outdoor adventure denied them, they will literally start climbing the walls! The only way for a Sagittarius to get through it is to treat the lockdown like an adventure itself, to seek out the activities they can do during this unique adventure. There are plenty of household and exercise activities that are possible during a lockdown that can keep the Sagittarius amused. Sure, it's not the same as being stuck up a mountain, but lockdown is an adventure of itself, and if the Sagittarius can keep that in the forefront of their mind, they might just make it through without resorting to actually climbing up the wall.

Capricorn: Capricorns, generally, should be okay surviving a lockdown. With their steadfast nature, they should have no problem complying with the rules, and they usually have a positive attitude to tasks, so it should be no different treating lockdown as just another task they have to get done. They just have to be careful with the people they are living with. Capricorns do have the tendency to treat partners and family like employees at times, so they need to be particularly mindful that during a lockdown, they don't start behaving like a sergeant in an army and ordering their partners and family around. If they can avoid that, they should be able to get through the lockdown just fine.

Aquarius: Lockdown is a bit of a mixed bag for Aquarians. They are known for being free-spirited, so being stuck at home isn't great for them. They also tend to like to rebel, so being told what to do by a government is going to be hard for them, particularly if they don't trust the government in the first place. But, there are positives for Aquarius, because they do like finding their own way, and so it will be with a lockdown. They will find their own way through it, coming up with unique ways of looking at things. They are another sign who may benefit from being in 2020 and having an online world they can profess to and be inspired by. Aquarians will not find it easy; they will long to be able to get out and roam about, but they will find their own unique way to cope with lockdown and do it well.

Pisces: Hmm, poor old Pisces. Just the fact people have to go into lockdown is more than this sensitive star sign can bear. Their empathetic and caring ways mean they are going to be worried about everybody and everything during this time. They will need to be aware of their mental health and make sure the world situation does not get on top of them. Their hankering for the old days is probably going to go into overtime during a lockdown. I think of all the signs, Pisces is going to find it the toughest to cope with. But, their empathetic nature means they can help out others during this time, which may keep their minds off worrying about the bigger picture. The thing for Pisces to keep in mind is that nothing lasts forever, not even a lockdown, not even a pandemic. If they can remember that, that is their best chance of surviving and possibly even thriving in a lockdown.

So, as you can see, being the star sign you are might just be the indicator as to whether you have got what it takes to survive a lockdown or whether you might be at risk of going under. We are all individuals, though, and we all have our own ways of dealing with things. What works for you works for you. Don't use this chapter as some kind of bible for you as to the correct way to survive a lockdown. That is not what it is; it is not a scientific or sociological document on human behavior. But, if you feel that you take on nearly all or all of the attributes of your star sign, hopefully this chapter will serve as a guide for you as to what you need to be extra careful and wary of, and if you've found the lockdown a complete breeze, then this has may have explained why that might be.

Personally, as a Virgo, I think I lived up to the stereotypical nature of a Virgo and found lockdown relatively easy to get through. I'm more nervous about post-lockdown than I was about the lockdown itself. During that time, I found I got on with all those creative things I just didn't seem to have the time (or perhaps motivation) for previously, like writing a novel, learning to play an instrument, and reading. Virgos do have a reputation for cleanliness, which I don't particularly agree with, but perhaps that is just because it is missing from me! I think this comes from the misinterpretation about Virgos being perfectionists, which I personally don't think they are. Anyway, I survived my own lockdown. Who knows? There might be more to come. I am confident that whatever your star sign, you will overcome any lockdowns you may face and the uncertainty of the world we are all living in at the moment, and having an insight to your star sign may help you understand why you are behaving like you are during these times.

It can also be useful to apply the thoughts in this chapter and others not just to the lockdown, but to any type of crisis, and think about how best it is for you to get through it. This could be the death of a loved one, illness, being caught up in someone else's emergency, or the threat of bankruptcy. In all these and many other situations where you are put under great stress and strain, it is worth considering how you think your personality would come out in such a situation, and what action you might need to take to make sure the worst excesses of that don't come out and play. We all have our own ways of dealing with things, and we all have our own outlets for getting rid of stress and anger, but in the current world where lots of those things might not be open to us, it is worth thinking about the safest and most mindful ways of dealing with critical situations, such as a pandemic and a lockdown. I hope this chapter has done that, and you can find your own peace and solace in the world right now, and not only have the tools to get through a lockdown, but to anything else we may face in the upcoming months and years.

Conclusion

If people were taking bets on what my opening line for the conclusion might have been, there will probably have been a few people who hit the jackpot. Astrology is not a science. Did you bet on that one? Well done if you did. But, it is important to reiterate that throughout this book. Astrology is fun, astrology is interesting, and I personally believe astrology can give you an insight into your personality and how you interact with other people and star signs, but what it is not is a science. There is little to no scientific evidence to back up any claims astrologists have ever made, and I want to be really clear about that.

However, astrology has been around for thousands of years, and there is a reason for that. A lot of it has to do with the human race's eternal desire to understand where we came from and what our purpose in the world and in the universe is—questions that can never probably be answered. While they can't be answered, humans wonder and dream. It's impossible to look up at the sky and not feel wonder and awe. This is why astrology began in the first place and why it is still going strong now even with ever-developing science and technology. But, it is also because when people look at their star signs and the characteristics that star sign takes on, and then they see how their star sign interacts with other star signs, they usually find a truth in that, and if not *a* truth, then their own truth. That is why astrology still succeeds when many others fail, and who are any of us to tell someone their truth is wrong?

The thing is, if you are looking at your star sign and your strengths and weaknesses, chances are you are looking at that because you want to know how to be a better person. You want to know how you can be better for other people, and you want to find what your purpose in life is. There is definitely nothing wrong with that, and while astrology is not a science, I believe it can be useful in helping you achieve those aims. Where I do become extremely concerned is if people start getting into daily horoscopes and actually defining their day and making any decisions based on what their horoscope says. That is a very dangerous path into which to go down. I believe it ends up creating a fear of life rather than encouraging an enjoyment of life. One of the few ways to learn is to make mistakes. If we never make mistakes, we rarely learn. I don't believe that trying to completely avoid making mistakes is the best route to go down, and that is what horoscopes and the like try to do. You end up making decisions based on your horoscope, when chances are whatever your gut was telling you was right in the first place. You don't need a horoscope to tell you whether to accept a job or not; you already know whether it is the best thing for you. If you follow through with believing everything in your daily horoscope, this also results in a kind of selfish and closed-off behavior. You stop listening to all that good advice from your friends and family who know you best. You stop listening to yourself. You only trust what the astrologer and horoscope says, and that is a very dangerous scenario to end up with. It is impossible to make the right choices in that situation.

Whatever other astrologers may say, nothing is predetermined. There is always some kind of choice you have to make. By all means, use astrology and star signs to help inform that choice, but don't rely on it, and definitely do not rely on a daily horoscope. You can use these things to help inform your choice, but there are a number of things you can use. Your own gut instinct still tells you a lot, as well as the reasoning you do in your mind. Trusted friends and family members, who have seen patterns of behavior from you before, can perhaps determine when you are heading for disaster quicker than you can. You can also carry out research and study from objective sources on any given number of topics and subjects. All these things can be used to help inform your choices in life. Don't only use or rely on astrology. If you do, don't blame it. One reason a person may want to follow astrology so closely and rely on an astrologer and/or a daily horoscope is so that they don't have to take responsibility for their life themselves. "Oh, it was my astrologer's fault, I made the wrong choice and now my life is miserable," "I followed my daily horoscope and yet I've had the worst day ever, it is all the horoscope's fault!" If only life were that simple. No, it was the person's fault. They are the ones who chose to follow that advice and refuse to listen to any other advice to their own detriment.

It also goes without saying that in the world of astrology, it is easy to fall prey to charlatans and fakes who masquerade as people who can predict the future and predict your life. They can't. Well, no more than anybody could. So, don't believe them. Even if you see a more believable astrologer who isn't silly enough to try to predict the apocalypse or what is going to happen to you in six days' time, but concentrates more on your star sign and your star sign characteristics and uses that to better guide what you should or shouldn't be doing, keep your eyes open. Don't just instantly believe what they tell you and get into that "they knew things about me I didn't even know myself" frame of mind. Possibly the reason you didn't know it about yourself is because it isn't true! Be careful, soak up what they say, take it away, and think about whether what they are saying is relevant to you and right for you to apply to your life or not. Those are all my warnings. Otherwise, I hope this book has given you a basic understanding and an enjoyment of astrology that you will take forward and, if relevant, look to apply to your life.

I hope I have given a good explanation of the history of astrology and what it means, and what the star signs and the attributes and characteristics associated with them are. Through these chapters, we have seen how those attributes and characteristics can be taken into consideration for dating and relationships, work, hobbies, health issues, and coping with a lockdown. These are just a few of the important areas I wanted to concentrate on, but there are many other areas, and now that I have translated the secret language of astrology to you, you can go away and practice fluently in any area of your life that you so wish to.

An important thing to remember is we are all individuals. Throughout this book, I have given examples of exceptions to rules and people who completely bucked the trend in terms of star sign behavior, such as the married Virgos who didn't seem to have any of the normal attributes of Virgos, or the Aquarian that I considered to actually have different attributes of Capricorn, Aquarius, and Pisces within them. I've also mentioned people that, at first glance, may not appear to have the traditional attributes associated with the star sign, but then when you look more deeply, they do. One was the Leo who seemed a very unassuming person, but then you realized the way they got attention and their own version of the spotlight was by being a soccer referee. Humans and human behavior is fascinating, and that is one of the many reasons astrology and star signs can be such fun to look into and follow. We still know so little about how the brain works, because if you take a brain out of a human to study, the human stops functioning, and you can't mess around with the brain while it is still in the human as it can have such a detrimental effect. So, seeing how humans behave and react to things is still such a great fascination to us and can leave us amazed and astounded. While that research is still continuing, astrology can be a useful way to think about human behavior and how humans react to and with each other.

It is also interesting how where you are born or live in the world tends to be the astrology you most identify with and follow. I briefly touched on Chinese and Indian astrology in the introduction, and if you are interested in astrology, it is well worth reading up on those two variations. What is strange is that, being a 'Westerner,' I identify with my Western zodiac sign, but when I look into my Chinese zodiac sign, which is a snake by the way, I just do not identify with it all. Yet, I don't share all the attributes of a Virgo either, so why do I identify with that sign so much more? It is the opposite with my wife, who is from Asia. She is an Aquarius in Western astrology, which I find she only has minimal attributes of, where her sign in Chinese astrology is (lucky her) a dragon, and I definitely see the dragon signs and qualities in her. How strange! There is a lot of work and research in unconscious bias these days. Is it actually my unconscious bias making me a Westerner identify with my Western sign and not my Chinese sign, but when it comes to my Asian wife, my unconscious bias makes me think she has more in common with her Chinese sign rather than her Western sign? Or maybe it is that in the formation of those astrologies the world was not as global as it is now, and so it was inevitable that the attributes of the star signs took on attributes of the peoples of those parts of the world. It is an interesting question worth pondering on. I don't have the answer, I'm just putting it out there for your consideration.

The aim of this book was to unlock the secret language of astrology and make you more knowledgeable about star signs, make you aware of how you can apply that knowledge to your life and to those around you, and improve your life for the better. I would hope I have done that, and you now feel super confident to go ahead and start improving your life in the areas I have concentrated on in this book, and in any other areas where you feel drastic improvement is needed. Congratulations, you are now fluent in the language of astrology. You can talk astrology with others fluent in the language, and you can even go and take a degree in it if you are so inclined. Have fun with it, be curious with it, but don't take it so seriously that you start to believe you can predict the end of the world or you turn down a lucrative job offer because your daily horoscope says not to accept any job offers for this month. Ruin lies down that road. Keep to star signs and star sign behavior and you should be able to enjoy applying it to your life. Life should become more enjoyable as a result.

References

Astrology, n.d. In Cambridge English Dictionary, Retrieved September 20, 2020, from https://dictionary.cambridge.org/dictionary/english/astrology

Astrology, n.d. In Oxford Language English Dictionary, Retrieved September 20, 2020 from https://www.google.co.uk/search?safe=strict&sxsrf=ALeKk0 2REfaZieGK7YmUxwGGpEPALD4J8g%3A1599644282464 &source=hp&ei=eqJYX7X7GMGMa- HWv5AJ&q=what+is+astrology%3F&oq=what+is+astrology %3F&gs_lcp=CgZwc3ktYWIQAzIECCMQJzICCAAyAggAM gIIADICCAAyAggAMgIIADICCAAyAggAMgIIADoKCAA QsQMQgwEQQzoLCC4QsQMQxwEQowI6BQgAELEDOg UIABCRAjoL

Best Life, *50 Mind-Blowing Horoscope Facts*, (2020), https://bestlifeonline.com/crazy-horoscope-facts/

Billington, Lara, *These are the careers for you based on your star sign*, GradTouch.com (2019, August 14), https://www.gradtouch.com/advice/article/content-careers- you-would-suit-based-on-your-star-sign

Cafe Astrology, *Timing With The Moon In Astrology*, (2020), https://cafeastrology.com/timingwiththemoon.html

Faragher, Aliza Kelly. *Each Zodiac Signs Unique Personality Traits*, Allure.com, (2020. August 31), https://www.allure.com/story/zodiac-sign-personality-traits- dates

Faragher, Aliza Kelly & Saint-Thomas, Sophie, *Zodiac Love Compatibility: Which Signs to Date—And Which to Avoid,* Allure.Com, (2020, February 12), https://www.allure.com/story/astrology-sign-love-compatibility

Fonseca, Silvia, *Interesting Facts About Astrology,* Amomedia, (2020, March 19), https://amomedia.com/187677-interesting-facts-about-astrology.html

Frank, Debbie, *Your zodiac star sign reveals how you're coping with lockdown.* Hello! Magazine.com, (2020, April 14), https://www.hellomagazine.com/news/2020041487961/how-your-star-sign-coping-in-lockdown/

Hess, Peter M.J. & Allen, Paul L. (2007). *Catholicism And Science,* (1st edition). Westport and Greenwood. ISBN 978-0-313-33190-9.

History World, *History of Astrology,* (2020), http://www.historyworld.net/wrldhis/plaintexthistories.asp?historyid=ac32

Judkis, Maura, *How app culture turned astrology into a modern obsession,* The Washington Post, (2019, November 20), https://www.washingtonpost.com/lifestyle/style/how-app-culture-turned-astrology-into-a-modern-obsession/2019/11/20/2d14e362-f9a7-11e9-8906-ab6b60de9124_story.html

Junction. Pundit, *Hobbies That Interests You According to Zodiac Signs,* Medium. Com, (2017, March 31), https://medium.com/@pjunction/hobbies-that-interests-you-according-to-zodiac-signs-44ec9ac386f

Kahn, Nina, *A Beginner's Guide to Understanding a Void Moon,* Bustle.com (2020, July 10), https://www.bustle.com/life/void-of-course-moon-astrology-meaning-explainer

Leo, Bessie & Besant, Annie, (1919). *The life and work of Alan Leo: Theosophist-Astrologer-Mason.* Metrology Office

Lily, William, (1681). *William Lily's history of his life and times.* T. Davies

Manning, Kathleen, *Should Catholics consult their horoscopes?*, U.S. Catholic, (2015, July 4), https://uscatholic.org/articles/201507/should-catholics-consult-their-horoscopes/

New World Encyclopedia, *Astrology*, (2020), https://www.newworldencyclopedia.org/entry/Astrology

Pixaby.com—all images.

Pochin, Courtney, *Horoscope app is sending weird notifications—and it's freaking them out*, The Daily Mirror (2019, March) https://www.mirror.co.uk/tech/horoscope-app-sending-people-weird-14195228

Taylor, Camelia, *The Purpose of Astrology*, (2014, August 19), https://www.purposeof.com.au/the-purpose-of-astrology/

Taylor Grant, Eva, *The One Health Problem Each Zodiac Sign Is Most Prone To,* Bustle.com (2018, June 13), https://www.bustle.com/p/the-one-health-problem-each-zodiac-sign-is-most-prone-to-9375561

The Chinese Zodiac, (2020), https://depts.washington.edu/triolive/quest/2007/TTQ07030/mythology.html

Vetal, Hyas, *Astrology Is A Science, Bombay HC,* The Times Of India, (2011, Feb, 3), https://timesofindia.indiatimes.com/india/Astrology-is-a-science-Bombay-HC/articleshow/7418795.cms